Grade 4

Wonders

Your Turn
Practice Book

McGraw Hill Education

www.mheonline.com/readingwonders

Mc Graw Hill Education

Send all inquiries to:
McGraw-Hill Education
Two Penn Plaza
New York, NY 10121

Printed in the United States of America.

7 8 9 10 11 12 QSX 22 21 20 19 18 B

Contents

Unit 1 • Think It Through

Contents

Unit 2 • Amazing Animals

Literary Lessons

Animals in Fiction

Natural Connections

Adaptations

Animals All Around

Contents

Unit 3 • That's the Spirit!

Friendship

Helping the Community

Liberty and Justice

Powerful Words

TIME For Kids

Contents

Unit 4 • Fact or Fiction?

Our Government

Leadership

Breakthroughs

Wonders in the Sky

Achievements

Contents

Unit 5 • Figure It Out

Contents

Unit 6 • Past, Present, and Future

Old and New

Notes from the Past

Resources

Money Matters

Finding My Place

Name ______________________________

gracious	flattened	muttered	brainstorm
stale	frantically	official	original

Finish each sentence using the vocabulary word provided.

1. **(gracious)** The young girl ______________________________

____

2. **(stale)** After two days ______________________________

____

3. **(flattened)** He always fixed his hair ______________________________

____

4. **(frantically)** After we got separated ______________________________

____

5. **(muttered)** I could not hear ______________________________

____

6. **(official)** After she won the cooking contest, ______________________________

____

7. **(brainstorm)** We all decided to ______________________________

____

8. **(original)** The second book he wrote ______________________________

____

Name ______________________________

Read the selection. Complete the sequence graphic organizer.

Character
Setting
Beginning
Middle
End

Name ______________________________

Read the passage. Use the make, confirm, or revise predictions strategy to predict what will happen in the story.

Coyote's Song

A boy was eating lunch in a field on his grandmother's farm.
12 Her farm was large and he had explored and seen many things that
25 morning. "Do not wander into the woods," Grandmother said. So he
36 kept to the fields. As he ate his lunch, he heard the call of a blue jay.
53 "I'll follow the sound of Blue Jay. I will find him and see his blue
68 feathers and listen to his song. I will bring him bread."
79 The afternoon sun was hot and there were many hills to climb,
91 but the boy was determined to follow the call. He walked slowly and
104 cautiously with care.
107 Soon he ran into Coyote who was looking for lunch but not having
120 any luck. He did not have a single crumb or morsel of food.
133 "Hello," said Coyote. "I see you are enjoying an afternoon walk."
144 "I've been exploring Grandmother's farm and now I'm looking for
154 Blue Jay. I want to listen to his song, see his beautiful feathers, and
168 give him bread."
171 Coyote took one look at the bread and became hungrier. Quietly,
182 he muttered to himself, "I will trick that boy, then he'll give me that
196 bread."
197 "I can sing a song and perform for you. Then you can give me your
212 bread," Coyote said with a grin.
218 "But howling and barking isn't a song, and you only have brown
230 fur," said the boy. "I want to hear Blue Jay's song and admire his
244 feathers, and I only have enough bread for him."

Name ______________________________

Coyote's original plan didn't work, so he quickly thought of a new one. "Then I'll help you find Blue Jay," said Coyote. "I know where he sings. I can take you there through the woods."

The boy remembered Grandmother's warning. What was the harm, the boy thought to himself. "Then let's go," said the boy.

"We must run! Blue Jay will depart soon and then he'll be gone," said Coyote. Coyote began running through the woods calling out for the boy to run faster and faster.

The boy did not want to miss Blue Jay, yet the faster he ran the more he stumbled and tripped on tree roots. The woods became thicker and thicker, making it harder for the boy to run.

Accustomed to running in the woods, Coyote was used to jumping over the roots so he didn't fall. "Hurry! Blue Jay and his song and feathers will leave!" said Coyote.

"You could run faster if you were not slowed down and burdened by having to carry that bread. I can carry it for you, and then you can run faster," said Coyote.

"If you think that will help," said the boy, "here is the bread."

Coyote took the bread in his mouth and disappeared.

"Thank you for the meal!" Coyote howled as he ate the bread.

The boy had been tricked, and now he was lost in the woods. By evening he found his way back to Grandmother's home and explained to her what happened.

"You should know that leaving the right path to follow an easier one leads to trouble," she said. "Luckily, you only lost some old, stale bread."

Name ______________________________

A. Reread the passage and answer the questions.

1. What are two events that happen after the boy hears Blue Jay?

____

____

____

2. Why is the setting of the woods important to the story?

____

____

____

3. Use the sequence of events to summarize the plot.

____

____

____

____

B. Work with a partner. Read the passage aloud. Pay attention to intonation. Stop after one minute. Fill out the chart.

	Words Read	–	Number of Errors	=	Words Correct Score
First Read		–		=	
Second Read		–		=	

Name ______________________________

Before the Ball

I waved my wand. Light flashed, and in a puff of smoke, the pumpkin transformed into a beautiful horse and carriage! I turned to Cinderella and smiled. "Not bad. What do you think?" I asked.

"It's perfect!" Cinderella shouted. "How can I ever repay you for all you have done?"

"You can get into that carriage and get to the ball on time!" I said, and sent her on her way.

Finally, Cinderella was off to the ball. My work was done.

Answer the questions about the text.

1. How do you know this story is a fairy tale?

It is made-up.

2. What events in the text identify it as a fairy tale?

You can not turn a pumpkin into a horse carrige.

3. What task does the main character have to complete? How does she complete it?

She completes cinderalla be a princess. She completes it by magic

4. What other text feature does "Before the Ball" include? How does it show that the story is a fairy tale?

The text feature is a picture

It shows you

Name same

Read the sentences below. Circle the synonym clue in the sentence that helps you understand the meaning of each word in bold. Then, in your own words, write the meaning of the word in bold.

1. It can be fun to **explore** all the rooms of a museum. You can discover things you have never seen.

   discover discover

2. The pilot told us the plane would **depart** in five minutes. We were glad it would leave on time.

   leave

3. The camel moved slowly, **burdened** by all packages it carried. People who saw the camel thought it was too loaded down.

   loaded

4. She **stumbled** into the room, tripping over the small step she had not seen in the doorway.

   tripping

5. It was the **howling** that frightened the campers. Never before had they heard such a loud barking sound in the woods.

   barking

6. My cousin got **accustomed** to sleeping late during the summer. It was hard for her to get used to waking up early once school started.

   hard used to

7. When it came time to **perform** for the judge, the singer was not nervous. He had been singing in contests since he was a child.

   contests

Name ______________________________

A. Read each sentence. Circle the word that has a short-vowel sound. Write the word on the line.

1. The strange bell always chimes so late! __________
2. My poor health was a good reason to stay home. __________
3. The tire was flat, so we needed to wait. __________
4. I could hear the crunch of the toy falling down the stairs. __________
5. She gave the team hints so they could find the clue. __________

B. Write the correct *-ed, -s,* and *-ing* forms for each verb.

Verb	+ *ed*	+ *s*	+ *ing*
1. float	__________	__________	__________
2. work	__________	__________	__________
3. start	__________	__________	__________
4. follow	__________	__________	__________
5. answer	__________	__________	__________

Name ____

A. Read the draft model. Use the questions that follow the draft to help you think about what descriptive details you can add.

Draft Model

Once there was a princess who lived in a castle. She was tired of climbing stairs. She asked her father for a platform she could stand on that would carry her from floor to floor. Today we call it an elevator.

1. When and where does this story take place?
2. What descriptive details can be added to help the reader visualize the princess?
3. Why was the princess tired of climbing stairs?
4. What descriptive details could provide more information about the elevator?

B. Now revise the draft by adding descriptive details that create a clearer picture of the princess, her father, and the elevator.

____

____

____

____

____

____

____

____

Name ______________________________

Kyle used text evidence from two different sources to respond to the prompt: *Add an event to the story. Describe what happens when Tomás visits Princess Paulina's Pizza Palace to sell some grapes. Use details from both stories.*

After a long, exhausting walk, Tomás and his son, Luis, were at their destination. Now finally standing inside Princess Paulina's Pizza Palace, Luis wearily dropped the giant burlap sack of grapes he had been carrying onto the counter. Then Paulina rushed out of the kitchen. "You're finally here! I've been waiting weeks for your juicy grapes to make a new kind of pizza for Queen Zelda," Paulina squealed.

"Yes, it was a long walk and we're very tired. But we would do anything to help you cook for the queen," replied Tomás.

Suddenly, Queen Zelda and Prince Drupert walked into the pizza shop for their weekly meal. Paulina introduced them to Tomás and Luis and then she ran back into the kitchen to start cooking the new style of pizza with grapes on top. While waiting for the pizza to cook, Luis took out his gourd drum and entertained the queen and prince with music. Finally, Paulina brought out the steaming, hot pizza covered in huge grapes and they all enjoyed it together.

Reread the passage. Follow the directions below.

1. **Circle** an example of dialogue in the story.

2. **Draw a box** around the descriptive details that Kyle uses to help the reader visualize the scene.

3. **Underline** sequence words that show the order of events in the story.

4. **Write** one of the exclamatory sentences that Kyle uses on the line.

____

Name ______________________________

accountable	desperately	humiliated	self-esteem
advise	hesitated	inspiration	uncomfortably

Finish each sentence using the vocabulary word provided.

1. **(desperately)** Even though the girl was very tired, ______________________________

____

2. **(self-esteem)** After the boy's team won a soccer game, ______________________________

____

3. **(inspiration)** The girl's amazing science fair project ______________________________

____

4. **(accountable)** The teacher told the students ______________________________

____

5. **(advise)** I know the dentist will ______________________________

____

6. **(uncomfortably)** During the summer, ______________________________

____

7. **(hesitated)** The child walked to the edge of the pool but ______________________________

____

8. **(humiliated)** At her dance performance, the girl ______________________________

____

Name ______________________________

Read the selection. Complete the problem and solution graphic organizer.

Character

teach Germer
Rod
Lucas friends

Setting

school

Problem

did not do essay

Event

will collect essay

Event

name expert

Solution

Finish this, wanted to have
be a name expert

Name ____

Read the passage. Use the make predictions strategy to check your understanding.

The Cyber Bully

Every time I got on the school bus, I felt sick and got butterflies in
15 my stomach. I had recently moved to a new school, and no one on the
30 bus talked to me. I was certain I would never make any new friends.
44 Right off the bat, the very first week of school, I was in deep trouble.
59 It all started when my teacher, Mr. Evers, took us to the computer
72 lab to do an assignment. I was logging in when I noticed my
85 classmate, Corey, watching my fingers on the keyboard. He looked at
96 me and smirked. I could tell something was wrong.
105 "I know your password, Aaron," Corey said.
112 "Um...ok," I said.
116 Right away he logged into his computer using my password!
126 I thought about telling Mr. Evers, but I didn't want the other kids to
140 think I was a tattle-tale. After all, I was the new kid, and I didn't
155 want to get off on the wrong foot or make a bad impression. I decided
170 to just focus on my work.
176 A few minutes later I heard Mr. Evers say, "Aaron? Could you
188 come here for a second?"
193 Just as I was getting up, I got a message. "You better keep your
207 mouth shut," it said. I couldn't tell who it came from since it was from
221 my own account.
225 "What is the meaning of this e-mail you sent me?" said Mr. Evers.
238 I read it but couldn't believe my eyes!
246 "But I haven't been on e-mail at all!" I said. Then I realized that it
261 was Corey using my e-mail!

Railwar
neighbor
obey

Name ____

"I...I..." I said. I felt like I was stuck between a rock and a hard place. I wanted desperately to tell the truth, but that would mean getting Corey into trouble. I worried about what the other students would think of me. I hesitated, thinking about what to do.

"I'm sorry," I said, deciding not to tell what happened.

"I'm giving you detention after school today," said Mr. Evers. He pulled out a pink detention slip and wrote my name on it. I felt humiliated as I walked back to my seat.

When the bell rang at the end of school, everyone got up from their desks to leave. I stayed behind to serve detention.

"Too bad," Corey laughed as he was leaving. Then it hit me. Corey would continue to bully me if I let him. I decided to be brave. I got up and walked over to Mr. Evers.

"Mr. Evers," I said. "I have something to tell you." I told him the whole truth about Corey stealing my password and using my account, and that I was sorry for not saying so earlier.

"I see," said Mr. Evers. "I would advise you to always tell the truth, Aaron, even if it means someone else might get in trouble. I will have a talk with Corey tomorrow."

I was still worried that the other students would be mad at me for telling Mr. Evers what Corey had done. But on the bus that afternoon a girl I recognized from my class sat next to me.

"I heard about what happened," she said softly. "You know you could have told us. No one should have to face a bully alone."

Another kid from my class turned around with a big grin on his face.

"Alana is right," the boy said. "We would have helped you. What are friends for? Hi, my name is Quentin."

Name ______________________________

A. Reread the passage and answer the questions.

1. What problem does Aaron face?

He got cyber bulled by cores

2. Why is Aaron worried about telling Mr. Evers the truth?

He does not want kids to think this was a taunatel teller.

3. What is the solution to Aaron's problem?

He told the teacher.

B. Work with a partner. Read the passage aloud. Pay attention to expression and rate. Stop after one minute. Fill out the chart.

	Words Read	–	Number of Errors	=	Words Correct Score
First Read		–		=	
Second Read		–		=	

Name ______________________

Paul's Mix-Up

"You're going to be at the show next week, right, Paul?" Rosa asked as the students packed up their instruments.

"Of course I am!" Paul said. "We've been practicing for months!"

Luis looked at Paul with curiosity. "You said you might not be able to make it. What about the trip you're taking with your family?"

Paul froze. All week long he had been thinking about their show. He had forgotten about his family trip!

Answer the questions about the text.

1. How can you tell this story is realistic fiction?

It is made up but can happen

2. What literary elements does the text include?

It has charters, plot

3. How does the dialogue make the story realistic?

Dialogue makes it realistic because their is no talking animals.

4. What details about Paul make him a believable character?

He talks and acks like a human.

Name ____

A. Read the idioms in the box. Find and underline an idiom in each sentence below. Then circle the context clues that help you understand the idiom.

butterflies in my stomach	between a rock and a hard place
right off the bat	get off on the wrong foot

1. Every time I got on the school bus, I felt sick, and got butterflies in my stomach. I had recently moved to a new school, and no one on the bus talked to me. I was certain I would never make any new friends.

2. Right off the bat, the very first week of school, I was in deep trouble.

3. I felt like I was stuck between a rock and a hard place. I wanted desperately to tell the truth, but that would mean getting Corey into trouble.

4. I didn't want to get off on the wrong foot or make a bad impression.

B. Read the sentences below. Underline each idiom. For each idiom, write a definition in your own words.

1. The test was a piece of cake because the questions were so easy.

It was very easy

____

2. He kept bothering me until I told him to cut it out.

to stop it

____

Name ______________________________

A. Circle the word with a long *a* vowel sound to complete each sentence. Then write it on the line to complete the sentence.

1. She had a big smile on her ________________.

   face hand fan

2. The show will begin at ________________ tonight.

   nine five eight

3. The drum ________________ marched with the band.

   major manner jam

4. My feet ________________ after walking so much!

   halt ache sleep

5. The cars stopped at the ________________ crossing.

   cattle railway street

B. Circle the correct form of the verb in the right column. Then match the verb in the left column to its correct form.

Verb	Verb + *-ed* or *-ing*
1. dive	createing / creating
2. shake	carved / carveed
3. believe	diving / diveing
4. create	shacking / shaking
5. carve	believeed / believed

Name ______________________________

A. Read the draft model. Use the questions that follow the draft to help you think about what details you can add about the central event.

Draft Model

Dan wanted to run for class president. He asked his friend to help him. He needed good ideas. "How about proposing a school-wide dance day?" his friend said, excitedly.

1. Why did Dan want to run for class president?
2. Why did he choose this friend to help him?
3. What does Dan think of the friend's idea?
4. What details would describe Dan's feelings and reactions?

B. Now revise the draft by adding details to help readers better understand and picture the event.

____

____

____

____

____

____

____

____

Name ______________________________

Petra used text evidence from two different sources to respond to the prompt: *Write a dialogue between Mrs. Greenberg and Rodney about Lucas being bullied at school. Use details from both sources.*

"Hello, Mrs. Greenberg. Can I talk to you about something?" I asked as I entered her empty classroom.

"Of course, Rodney. What is it?" Mrs. Greenberg replied.

"I wanted to tell you that Lucas is being bullied by other students. They always make fun of his name and call him Mucus. I don't like seeing him get upset when this happens."

"Oh, no. I was not aware of this. How does Lucas react to it?" she asked.

"He keeps his head down and ignores it. That works. But I am terrified that these students will soon start pushing him around. It makes me so nervous that I get hives on my neck," I said while wincing and rubbing my neck.

Mrs. Greenberg stood up and said, "Well, thank you, Rodney, for telling me about this. Ignoring them or using humor is a good way of defeating bullies. But bullying takes many forms and none of them are okay. I'll speak to the principal and talk to Lucas."

Reread the passage. Follow the directions below.

1. **Circle** the sentence that tells the event Rodney wants to talk about.

2. **Underline** the dialogue that tells you who Mrs. Greenberg is going to speak to.

3. **Draw a box** around an example of precise language.

4. **He keeps his head down and ignores it.**
   Write the subject in this sentence on the line below.

   ____

Name ______________________________

alter	collapse	destruction	severe
substantial	unpredictable	hazard	crisis

Finish each sentence using the vocabulary word provided.

1. **(alter)** When she saw that it was going to rain, ______________________________

____

2. **(collapse)** The fort we made of sticks was so fragile, ______________________________

____

3. **(destruction)** When the tidal wave hit the trees on the beach, ______________________________

____

4. **(severe)** The show was interrupted ______________________________

____

5. **(substantial)** Having to rebuild after the storm ______________________________

____

6. **(unpredictable)** We tried to catch the firefly, ______________________________

____

7. **(hazard)** When our neighborhood flooded, ______________________________

____

8. **(crisis)** When all the lights went out in town, ______________________________

____

Name ____

Read the selection. Complete the compare and contrast graphic organizer.

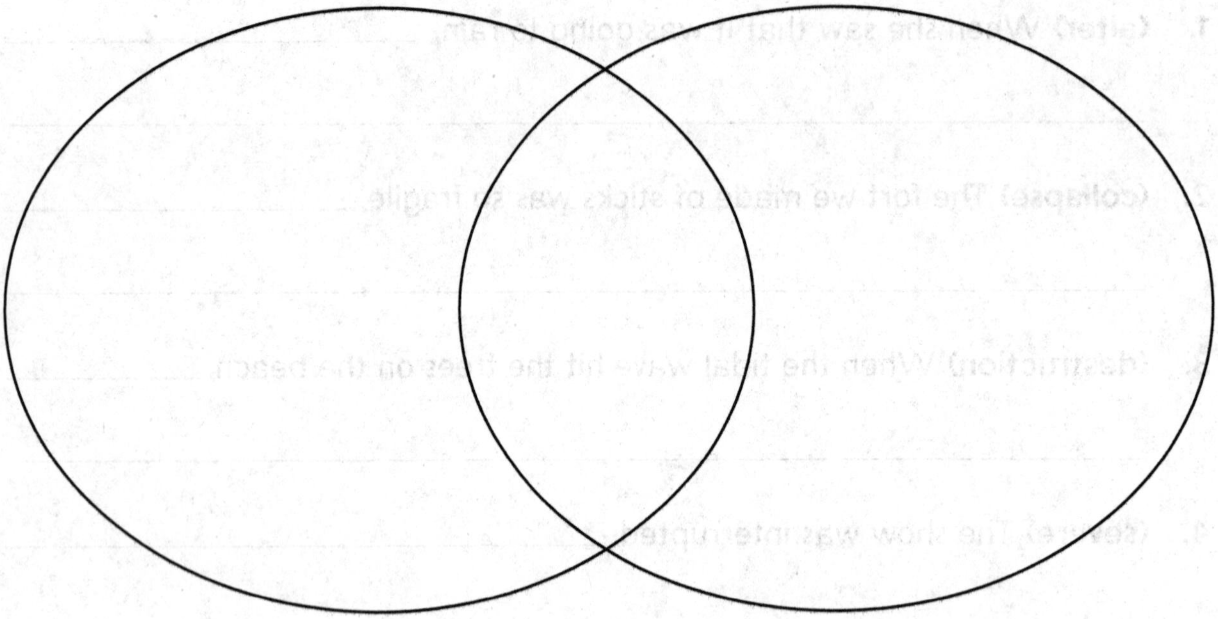

Name ______________________________

Read the passage. Use the reread strategy to check your understanding.

Rising Waters

Have you ever been in an earthquake or a tornado? These things
12 may never happen where you live. But flooding is something that can
24 happen in almost every part of the United States. Not all floods are
37 alike. Some floods happen over many days. A flash flood can happen
49 in minutes. Learning about floods can help you stay safe.

59 **Why Do Floods Happen?**

63 There are two types of floods. The first type happens when a river
76 has too much water. The water in a river rises over the river's banks.
90 This might happen because storms have caused too much rain to fall.
102 In rivers near mountains, melting snow can also cause floods. Warm
113 weather can quickly melt the snow. The water flows down to flood
125 the rivers.
127 The second type of flood happens when seawater is pushed onto
138 the land. This can happen during a hurricane. Strong winds blow
149 water onto the land. Earthquakes can also cause this kind of flooding.
161 The sudden movement of the ground can cause walls of water to rush
174 toward the shore.

Name ____________________

What Happens Next?

There can be many problems after a flood. If a farm floods, the water can drown the crops. This means that there will be less food for people to eat. Floods also cause damage to buildings and bridges. They can even wash away entire roads! This can make it hard for rescue workers to help people who are trapped by the water. But it is important to get food and drinking water to people during a flood. Everything they own may have been washed away. Or it might be covered in dirt. Sewers can overflow and make drinking water dirty. This makes it unsafe. Without clean food and water, people can get sick.

How Do People Avoid Floods?

All over the world, people work to avoid flooding. In many countries, people build walls to keep water away from the land. In one part of England, there is a large metal wall across a river. The wall is raised when the sea level gets too high. This keeps the river from flooding.

Photo by Lynn Betss, courtesy of USDA Natural Resources Conservation Service

In the United States, many towns have sold part of their land. The government used that land to create wetlands. These wetlands act like sponges that absorb water from floods. This helps stop the water from reaching towns and damaging them.

Floods can be scary, but flooding does not last forever. People are working to make floods less harmful to buildings, land, and themselves. Knowing how floods happen can help keep you safe. Being ready can help you stay safe too.

Name ____

A. Reread the passage and answer the questions.

1. What are the two things being compared in the second and third paragraphs?

____

____

____

2. What do these two things have in common?

____

____

____

3. How are these two things different?

____

____

____

B. Work with a partner. Read the passage aloud. Pay attention to accuracy. Stop after one minute. Fill out the chart.

	Words Read	–	Number of Errors	=	Words Correct Score
First Read		–		=	
Second Read		–		=	

Name ____________________

Forest Fires

Forest fires start and spread in different ways. The type of fire and the plants affect how it spreads. There are three types of forest fires. The first is a ground fire. It moves along the ground, sometimes below the leaf cover. Dead plant matter along the ground can burn for weeks and months. In a surface fire, low plants, twigs, and rotten logs catch fire. The flames can sometimes become tall and spread. The third type is a crown fire. It burns and spreads across the tops of trees and can be carried by the wind.

Answer the questions about the text.

1. How do you know this is an expository text?

It is not made-up.

2. What text features does the text include?

____

3. What is the heading of this text? How could it be made more specific?

The heading is Forest fires and a better one mait be 3 the forest fires.

4. What does the diagram show? How does it add to the text?

The different betence the 3 forest fires. It shows the fires

Name ____

Read each passage. Underline the context clues that help you figure out the meaning of each multiple-meaning word in bold. Then write the word's meaning on the line.

1. Have you ever been in an earthquake or a tornado? These things may never happen where you live. But flooding is something that can happen in almost every **part** of the United States.

a froiction of something

2. Not all floods are alike. Some floods happen over many days. A **flash** flood can happen in minutes. Learning about floods can help you stay safe.

very fast

3. Floods also cause damage to buildings and bridges. They can even **wash** away entire roads! This can make it hard for rescue workers to help people who are trapped by the water.

____

____

4. The water in a river rises over the river's **banks**. This might happen because storms have caused too much rain to fall.

____

____

Name ______________________________

A. Read the words in each row. Circle the word with the long *e* vowel sound. Then write the letters that make the long *e* sound on the line.

1. league large growl ______
2. deck sled sleek ______
3. scheme shelf sky ______
4. marked maybe melted ______
5. claim dense honey ______
6. farming family laying ______

B. Write the correct plural form of each noun. Use the plural ending *-s, -es,* or *-ies.*

Noun	Plural Form
1. kiss	______________
2. zebra	______________
3. buddy	______________
4. match	______________
5. stone	______________
6. box	______________

Name ____

A. Read the draft model. Use the questions that follow the draft to help you think about what supporting details you can add.

Draft Model

The park near my house is a great place to spend time. Many people enjoy hiking or walking in the park and looking at nature. The park has baseball fields.

1. Why is the park a great place?
2. What details would show what the park looks like?
3. What kinds of plants and animals might be in the park?
4. What do the baseball fields add to the park?

B. Now revise the draft by adding supporting details that help readers learn more about the park.

____

____

____

____

____

____

____

____

Name ____________________

Sara used text evidence from two different sources to answer the question: ***How do natural disasters affect people's lives?***

Earthquakes and tornadoes are both natural disasters that affect people's lives. When an earthquake happens, buildings may collapse. People in these buildings may get hurt, and some may lose their homes. This happens to people whose homes are near faults in the Earth's crust. The author says that the crust is like a "jigsaw puzzle." When these puzzle pieces move, an earthquake happens. Most earthquakes are small and harmless, but larger ones cause a lot of damage.

Tornadoes can cause a lot of damage, too. They are shaped like funnels. They seem to come out of the blue, and they race over the ground. The wind in a tornado is very strong. It can rip apart buildings, and it can pull trees right out of the ground. Finding a safe shelter helps people survive tornadoes. Homes hit by a tornado may be destroyed, and cars may blow through the air. Many people are injured by flying objects blown around by the tornado.

Reread the passage. Follow the directions below.

1. **Circle** the supporting detail that tells why some people lose their homes in an earthquake.

2. **Underline** a sentence that shows a comparison is being made.

3. **Draw a box** around an example of an idiom.

4. **Write** one sentence that Sara wrote that is a compound sentence.

____

____

Name ______________________________

thrilling	capabilities	friction	gravity
accelerate	inquiry	identity	advantage

Finish each sentence using the vocabulary word provided.

1. **(friction)** I use the brakes on my roller skates ______________________________

____

2. **(identity)** The policeman asked me ______________________________

____

3. **(thrilling)** At the amusement park, the roller coaster ______________________________

____

4. **(advantage)** The fact that the basketball player is very tall ______________________________

____

5. **(gravity)** The apple fell from the tree ______________________________

____

6. **(accelerate)** When traveling downhill, ______________________________

____

7. **(inquiry)** I used the Internet ______________________________

____

8. **(capabilities)** My friend is good at math and English ______________________________

____

Name ____

Read the selection. Complete the cause and effect graphic organizer.

Cause	→	**Effect**
	→	
	→	
	→	
	→	

Name ______________________________

Read each sentence below. Underline the context clues in the sentence that help you define each word in bold. Then, in your own words, write the definition of the word.

1. Charlie walked over to the **fire pole,** a metal pole which ran through a hole in the floor and connected the two levels of the firehouse.

____

2. **Inertia** means that an object at rest tends to stay at rest.

____

3. "A **force** is something that moves, stops, or changes the motion of an object," he said.

____

4. **Speed** is the distance an object moves in a certain amount of time.

____

5. **Gravity** is the force that pulls objects toward each other.

____

Name ____

A. Read each sentence. Underline the word with the long *i* vowel sound. Then sort the words by their long *i* spellings in the chart below.

1. Which of these is a prime number?

2. Make a slight turn at the next street.

3. She was minding the baby for you.

Long *i* spelled *i*	Long *i* spelled *i_e*	Long *i* spelled *igh*
4.	5.	6.

B. Write the correct *-es* and *-ed* forms for each verb ending in *y*.

Verb	+ *es*	+ *ed*
1. cry	____________	____________
2. fry	____________	____________
3. apply	____________	____________
4. deny	____________	____________
5. worry	____________	____________

Name ______________________________

A. Read the draft model. Use the questions that follow the draft to help you think about how you can write an event sequence that unfolds naturally.

Draft Model

We went to a dairy farm. We saw a farmer milk a cow. He showed us how he turns milk into butter. We learned how cheese is made from milk.

1. When did the writer go to the dairy farm?
2. What did the writer do first?
3. What time-order word would tell when the farmer showed the writer how he turns milk into butter?
4. What time-order word would tell when the writer learned how cheese is made from milk?

B. Now revise the draft by adding time-order words that help readers better understand the writer's trip to the dairy farm.

____

____

____

____

____

____

____

____

Name ______________________________

Henry wrote the paragraphs below using text evidence from two different sources to answer the prompt: *Compare how Max Axiom and the robots explain force and motion. Use details from* Force and Motion with Max Axiom, Super Scientist *and* "The Box-Zip Project."

The characters in both stories explain how force and motion work. In the graphic novel, *Force and Motion with Max Axiom, Super Scientist,* a scientist takes readers on a tour of an amusement park and a skateboard park. In "The Box-Zip Project," two robots fly to Earth and other planets in a machine.

To show what motion is, Max Axiom bungee jumps off a platform. The illustrations also give information. For example, a man chases a runaway stroller and uses force to stop it by grabbing the handle.

In "The Box-Zip Project," the two robots use force to move the Box-Zip across the floor and then to stop it. Shine, one of the robots, "held out his enormous robot hand and immediately stopped the sliding Box-Zip."

Both stories have characters that help readers understand how force and motion work.

Reread the passage. Follow the directions below.

1. **Circle** the text evidence that tells what the author's purpose is for writing these paragraphs.

2. **Draw a box** around the word in the first sentence that signals a comparison is being made.

3. **Underline** text evidence that shows how Max Axiom explains what motion is.

4. **Write** one of the complex sentences Henry uses on the lines.

____

____

Name ______________________________

process	routine	undertaking	compassionate
funds	enterprise	exceptional	innovative

Use a word from the box to answer each question. Then use the word in a sentence.

1. What is another word for *a regular series of actions*? ____________

____

2. What is a sum of money set aside for something? ____________

____

3. What word might describe something that is out of the ordinary?

____

4. What is another word for *something someone decides to do or start*?

____

5. What word might describe someone who cares about other people?

____

6. What is another word for *a difficult project*? ____________

____

7. What word might describe the steps you take to perform a task?

____

8. What word might describe someone who is likely to introduce new ideas?

____

Name ______________________________

Read the selection. Complete the main idea and details graphic organizer.

Main Idea
Detail
Detail
Detail

Name ______________________________

Read the passage. Use the reread strategy to help you understand the most important ideas in the passage.

A Helping Hand

Do you like to help others? Helping out is an important part of
13 being in a community. There are many others who feel the same way.
26 Helping can truly make a difference in a lot of ways. It is something
40 you can do every day. Make a Difference Day is one day a year that
55 reminds us how great it is to help others.
64 We should all be active and make a difference to better our community.
77 There is always a way to make a difference. Sometimes it is giving food
91 to someone who needs a meal. Sometimes it is a cleaning a local park.
105 Make a Difference Day is a good time to get others involved. It is a
120 great time to get your friends to help you make a difference, too.

133 **Clean a Park**

136 Making a difference is about helping. It is also a good way to learn.
150 If you and your friends clean a park, you can study plant life there.
164 You might see animals you have studied. So while cleaning, you have
176 learned about plants and animals. You have also made the park a
188 cleaner place for them and for you.

195 **Meet New People**

198 It is helpful to clean your community. But it is also good to meet
212 the people who live there. You can easily learn about other people
224 who live near you. Just talking to someone can make a difference. You
237 and your classmates can visit a senior citizen center. Ask the people
249 there about their lives. They will gladly tell you what it was like when
263 they were your age. This makes a difference by showing you care. It
276 also helps you get to know other people in your community.

Name ____

Feed Someone in Need

Do you know how important a good meal is? Some people aren't able to have a good meal every day. Make a difference by collecting food for them. You and your friends can work as a team to collect food. Choose a food bank you would like to help. Work together to collect food donations from your friends and your community. Then give the food to the food bank. They will be grateful for your help. This is something you can do all year round. It not only helps people in need. It also helps you and your friends know what teamwork is.

Be Creative

Cleaning parks, meeting new people, and giving food are good. There is also something you can do with your creativity. You and your friends can make an activity book. How is this making a difference? There are children who might not have these books. Your teacher can make copies. Then your team can distribute them. Take them to places like clinics or hospitals. There are children there who would like these books. It is a book that you and your team created together. More importantly it is a book that made the day better for a child.

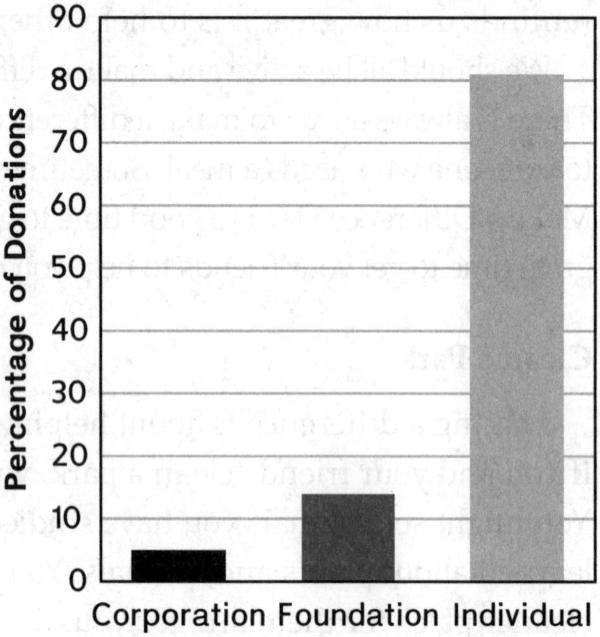

This graph shows where donations came from in North America in 2010. You can see that individuals like you give the most.

Making a difference is good. And Make a Difference Day is a good time to start. Making a difference can show you parts of your community you did not know about. You can meet new people and learn new things. Most of all, you can make a difference.

Name ____

A. Reread the passage and answer the questions.

1. What are three key details in paragraph 5?

____

____

____

2. How are these details connected?

____

____

____

3. What is the main idea of the whole passage?

____

____

____

B. Work with a partner. Read the passage aloud. Pay attention to phrasing and rate. Stop after one minute. Fill out the chart.

	Words Read	–	Number of Errors	=	Words Correct Score
First Read		–		=	
Second Read		–		=	

Name ______________________________

Donating to a Charity

Once your business starts making money, it's important to find a way to give back to the community. For instance, 9-year-old Jason O'Neill started a pencil topper business. After a few years of success, he decided to use some money to buy toys for a local children's hospital. In addition, he began holding an annual teddy bear drive so that others could help the hospital. Jason is a good example of a responsible businessperson.

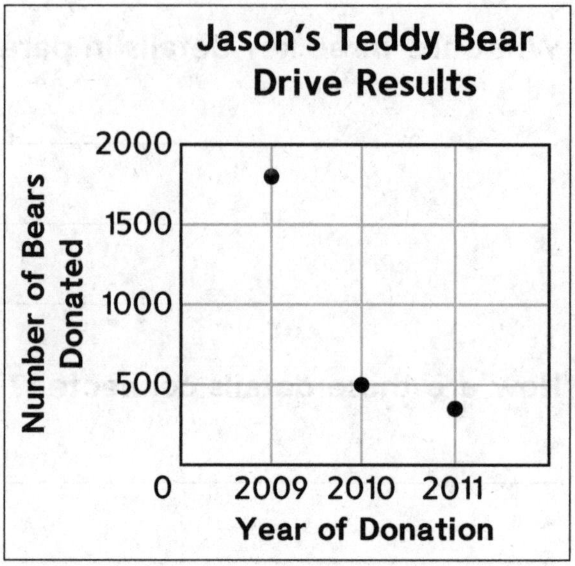

Answer the questions about the text.

1. How do you know this text is a persuasive article?

____

____

2. What text feature is included? What information does it show?

____

____

3. What is the heading of this article?

____

4. What does the author think about the article's subject?

____

____

Name ______________________________

Read each sentence below. Underline the suffix of the word in bold and write the word's definition on the line. Then write your own sentence using the word in bold.

1. Helping can **truly** make a difference in a lot of ways.

____

____

____

2. We should all be **active** and make a difference to better our community.

____

____

____

3. They will **gladly** tell you what it was like when they were your age.

____

____

____

4. They will be **grateful** for your help.

____

____

____

Name ______________________________

A. Read each sentence. Circle the word that has the long-vowel sound /ō/. Write the letter or letters that make the long-vowel sound /ō/ on the line.

1. Use the crane to lower the lumber to the ground. ____________
2. The bolt of lightning shot across the sky. ____________
3. The sad movie filled us all with woe. ____________
4. My shadow stays behind me when I walk down the stairs. ____________
5. Do you smell the chicken roasting in the oven? ____________
6. My favorite quote is from that great author. ____________

B. Read the words in the box. Mark the words that are not compound words with an *X*. Then list the compound words on the lines below.

workout	hunter	hands-on	childlike
catching	afternoon	half sister	weekend

1. ____________ 4. ____________

2. ____________ 5. ____________

3. ____________ 6. ____________

Name ____

A. Read the draft model. Use the questions that follow the draft to help you think about using sentences of different lengths to add interest and rhythm.

Draft Model

I think our community needs a frozen yogurt store. We have too many ice cream stores. Frozen yogurt is a healthy alternative to ice cream.

1. What sentences have related ideas that could be combined into a longer sentence?
2. What short sentences would you add to draw attention to the idea that frozen yogurt is a healthy alternative to ice cream?
3. What sentence would you add after the last sentence to help explain what it means? Would you make that sentence long or short to add rhythm?

B. Now revise the draft by using sentences of different lengths to add interest and rhythm.

____

____

____

____

____

____

____

____

Name ______________________________

Kendall wrote the paragraphs below from two different sources to answer the question: *In your opinion, how does learning about kids who started businesses and tips for starting a business help kids who want to become entrepreneurs?*

I think learning about kids who started businesses and tips for starting a business will help kids who want to be entrepreneurs. One article tells about businesses kids have started. The other article provides steps to follow as kids start their own business. Anyone can start a business!

In "Kids in Business," readers learn about kids who have started businesses. For example, Hayleigh turned her idea for charms that hang from hearing aids into a business. She now sells more than 50 different styles. Joshua works to feed people in need, and Cecilia raises money for charity.

"Starting a Successful Business" gives steps that kids who want to become entrepreneurs can follow. Steps 1 and 2 discuss having an innovative idea and figuring out if the idea can be turned into a successful business. These steps give important information such as where a product will be sold and to whom.

I think both these articles will help kids who want to become entrepreneurs.

Reread the passage. Follow the directions below.

1. **Circle** the shortest sentence in the first paragraph.

2. **Draw a box** around the text evidence that shows that Hayleigh's business is successful.

3. **Underline** two steps that kids who want to become entrepreneurs can follow.

4. **Write** the linking word in the second paragraph that combines two shorter sentences into a single, longer sentence.

____

Name ____

attracted	fabric	honest	soared
dazzling	greed	requested	trudged

Use the context clues in each sentence to help you decide which vocabulary word fits best in the blank.

Flying high in the air, Eagle ____________________ over the forest. Something drew his attention in the forest below and he flew down to see it. It was something colorful that had ____________________ him. When Eagle landed on the forest floor, he saw a splendid piece of cloth with bright, ____________________ colors.

He knew that the cloth might belong to someone else, but he had always desired just such a scarf. ____________________ got the best of him, and he picked up the piece of ____________________. Just then, Big Bear appeared, walking slowly toward Eagle. Big Bear ____________________ up next to him.

"Can you help me find my scarf?" Big Bear ____________________. At first, Eagle thought about hiding the scarf. But instead of lying, he decided to be ____________________. "Oh, well," thought Eagle. He handed the scarf to Big Bear and flew away.

Name ____

Read the selection. Complete the theme graphic organizer.

Detail

Detail

Detail

Theme

Name ______________________________

Read the passage. Use the ask and answer questions strategy to help you understand the folktale.

Anansi and His Children

Anansi was a spider who had six children, each with his or her
13 own special ability. The first child was named See Trouble, because
24 he could perceive trouble from far away. The next was Road Builder,
36 followed by River Drinker, Game Skinner, and Stone Thrower. The
46 last child was named Cushion, because he was so very soft. They
58 were all good children who loved Anansi.
65 Anansi was curious about the world and liked nothing more than to
77 travel. He loved to explore places far from home, but one day Anansi
90 became lost! Back at home, See Trouble knew at once what had
102 happened.
103 "Brothers and sisters!" said See Trouble. "Come quickly. Father is
113 lost. We must help him find his way back home."
123 Road Builder stepped forward, strong and sure-handed. "I will
132 build a road that will lead us to our father," Road Builder said, and
146 he began to construct a road. The other five children followed Road
158 Builder down the road as he worked. They trudged on and on until
171 finally they came to a mighty river. But, hard as they tried, they could
185 not see their father.
189 "Brothers and sisters," See Trouble cried. "I know why we do not
201 see our father. He has been swallowed by Big Fish!"
211 "It's a good thing I'm so thirsty," said River Drinker as she walked
224 to the river's edge and put her lips to the water. With gulp after
238 enormous gulp, she drank every drop of water in the river. There in
251 the mud sat Big Fish. Now it was Game Skinner's turn to help. She cut
266 open Big Fish, and Anansi crawled out, free at last!

Name ______________________________

But the danger was not over. Falcon swooped down from the sky, grabbed Anansi and soared into the clouds.

"Quickly, Stone Thrower!" yelled See Trouble. Taking careful aim, Stone Thrower hit Falcon with a stone. Anansi began to fall. Seeing this, Cushion ran to catch his father. Anansi landed on Cushion with a nice soft bounce, and Anansi was safe! The children cheered, happy to be with their father again.

On the way home, Anansi was attracted to something glowing in the woods. Always curious, he walked toward the glow and found something beautiful. It was a dazzling globe of light.

"Such a wonderful thing!" exclaimed Anansi. "I know just what I will do with it. I will give it to one of my children. But which one should I give it to?"

Seeking help, Anansi called to Nyame, who lived in the sky watching over all living things.

"I found this beautiful globe of light, Nyame. Will you hold it for me while I decide which child I should give it to?" Anansi asked.

"Gladly," said Nyame, and she reached down carefully to take the globe in hand. As she did so, a soft light fell on the forest.

Anansi went to his children and told them about the ball of light. All night long they argued over which one should receive the gift. Nyame watched from above as the argument went on and on.

It seemed they would never make a decision. So Nyame came to a decision of her own. Instead of giving the globe back to Anansi, Nyame placed it high above for every living thing to see. And that is the story of how the moon came to live in the sky.

Name ____

A. Reread the passage and answer the questions.

1. Pick one of Anansi's children to write about. Write the name of the character and explain how he or she uses his or her ability to save Anansi.

____

____

____

2. What is the decision Nyame comes to at the end of the story?

____

____

3. What is one of the themes of this story?

____

____

____

B. Work with a partner. Read the passage aloud. Pay attention to expression. Stop after one minute. Fill out the chart.

	Words Read	–	Number of Errors	=	Words Correct Score
First Read		–		=	
Second Read		–		=	

Name ______________________________

The Tiger, the Brahmin, and the Jackal

The jackal said to the Brahmin, "I understand that you agreed to let the tiger free if the tiger agreed not to eat you." He turned to the tiger. "And I understand that as soon as you were free, you said you would eat the Brahmin anyway. But I still can't understand this cage here..."

The tiger snarled impatiently. "Foolish jackal! How many times do I have to explain it?" he said. He walked into the cage to demonstrate how it worked. As soon as he was inside, the jackal closed the door behind him and locked him in.

The jackal turned to the Brahmin. "I think you should leave this cage closed," he said.

Answer the questions about the text.

1. How do you know this text is a folktale?

____

2. What literary elements are included in a folktale?

____

3. Choose a character. What quality do you think this character symbolizes?

____

____

4. What lesson do you think this folktale teaches?

____

____

Name ____

Read each passage below. Write the root word and the definition of the word in bold.

1. Anansi was a spider who had six children, each with his or her own special **ability**.

Root word: ______________

Definition: ____

2. "Such a **wonderful** thing!" exclaimed Anansi. "I know just what I will do with it. I will give it to one of my children. But which one should I give it to?"

Root word: ______________

Definition: ____

3. "Gladly," said Nyame, and she reached down **carefully** to take the globe in hand.

Root word: ______________

Definition: ____

4. Nyame watched from above as the **argument** went on and on.

Root word: ______________

Definition: ____

Name ____

A. Read each sentence. Circle the words that have prefixes. Then write the words with prefixes on the line.

1. I had to relearn the lesson because my answers were incorrect.

____

2. The imperfect lock made it difficult to unchain the bike.

____

3. I did not understand how his room could be so unclean and in such disorder!

____

4. The unhappy customer had to repeat that his meal was uncooked.

____

5. The shirt was an irregular shape and caused discomfort.

____

B. Write the correct *-ed* and *-ing* forms for each verb.

Verb	Verb + *ed*	Verb + *ing*
1. flap	____________	____________
2. drag	____________	____________
3. grin	____________	____________
4. scrub	____________	____________
5. admit	____________	____________

Name ______________________________

A. Read the draft model. Use the questions that follow the draft to help you think about how you can create a strong opening by adding details.

Draft Model

A man met a fox. The fox asked the man for help. The man had to decide if he wanted to help the fox. Both the fox and the man waited while the man decided if he would help the fox.

1. Who is the man? Where does he meet the fox?
2. What is the problem that the fox has?
3. What details would explain how the man could help the fox?
4. Why is the man trying to decide if he will help the fox?

B. Now revise the draft by creating a strong opening by adding details.

____

____

____

____

____

____

____

____

Name ______________________________

Marc wrote the paragraphs below using text evidence from two different sources to respond to the prompt: *Write a letter from the merchant to Gordi Goat in which the merchant explains why he did not save the goat. Use details from both stories.*

Dear Gordi Goat,

I was heading home from India when suddenly I heard a desperate crying sound coming from a well. I looked in and saw you, and I knew you were in bad shape. My helpers were carrying sacks of spices, so they could not help you. Besides, we had no rope to throw down to you and I had to get to the next town to buy more fabric.

However, when we got to the next town, I told people that you were stuck in a well. No one would go to the well and rescue you. Frankly, I think they thought it was your fault that you let the fox trick you.

I hope you understand that I am a busy and successful merchant. You really could not expect me to take the time to help you. After all, time is money. I am sure everything worked out well in the end.

Sincerely,
Persian Merchant

Reread the passage. Follow the directions below.

1. **Circle** the phrase that makes the reader want to know what happens next.
2. **Underline** the text that uses a transition word.
3. **Draw a box** around text evidence that helps you make an inference about what is important to the merchant.
4. **Write** three proper nouns that Marc uses on the lines below.

____

____

Name ____

cranky	frustrated	selfish	commotion
annoyed	specialty	attitude	familiar

Finish each sentence using the vocabulary word provided.

1. **(specialty)** The bakery is known for ______________________________
____.

2. **(frustrated)** When I couldn't figure out the multiplication problem, ________
____.

3. **(commotion)** We heard the two dogs barking loudly ______________________
____.

4. **(annoyed)** The cat saw the bird on the other side of the window ________
____.

5. **(attitude)** The boy is always ready to help __________________________
____.

6. **(selfish)** When I have a secret, ________________________________
____.

7. **(familiar)** When I heard the song on the radio, ______________________
____.

8. **(cranky)** When my baby sister is tired, __________________________
____.

Name ______________________________

Read the selection. Complete the theme graphic organizer.

Clue

↓

Clue

↓

Clue

↓

Theme

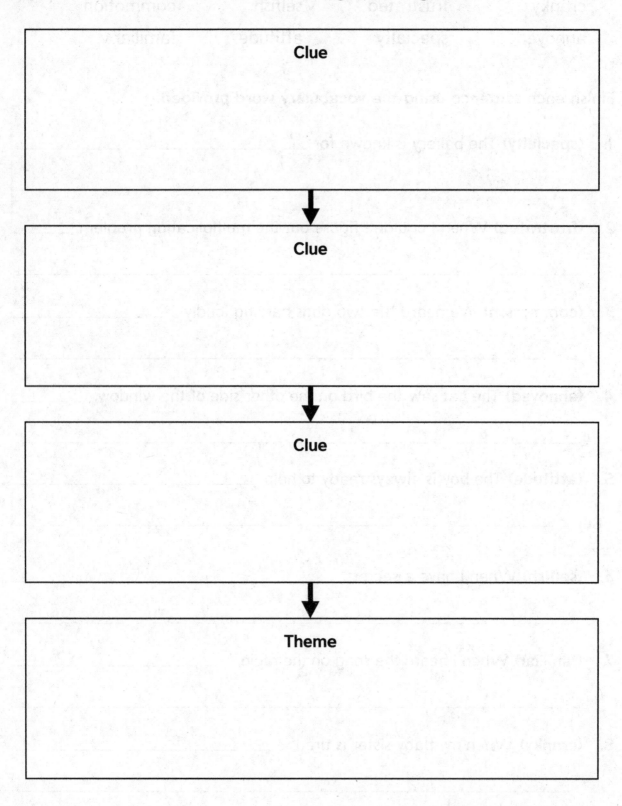

Name ____

Read the passage. Use the ask and answer questions strategy to be sure you understand what you read.

Grant and the Flower Stem

List of Characters

3 Grant, an ant
6 Beatrice, a bee
9 Frank, a bee

12 **Setting**

13 A field in Kansas.
17 *Grant has wandered away from his work and has fallen asleep. The*
29 *next morning, he climbs to the top of a sunflower stem and finds a*
43 *small house made of beeswax. No one is home.*

52 **Grant:** *(whispering)* What is this place? It looks like my house, but
64 everything is smooth and shiny! Everything in my house
73 is made of dirt and so rough. Oh man, I would love to live
87 here!
88 *(Beatrice walks in the door behind him.)*
95 **Beatrice:** *(yelling)* Who are you? And, more importantly, what are you
106 doing here?
108 **Grant:** I'm so sorry. My name is Grant. I just saw the stem to your
123 house and climbed up. I didn't know what I would find. But
135 your house is lovely! (*Cowering*) Please don't sting me!
144 **Beatrice:** *(laughs)* It's nice to meet you. Stand up straight and tall. I
157 haven't stung anyone in years, not unless they deserved it.

Name ____

Grant: That's a relief. I have heard stories about little ants that wander away and are stung by bees. I hear bees are very cranky.

Beatrice: Goodness no. It takes a lot to get me irritated. Someone has to be very unpleasant to make me a grouch. I am usually very friendly. You should watch out for my husband, however; he is grumpier than I am.

Grant: Is he going to sting me?

Beatrice: My goodness, Grant, you are one nervous ant. You shouldn't worry so much. He won't sting you.

Frank: *(Enters, but doesn't see Grant)* Good afternoon, Beatrice! Whose turn is it to make soup? *(Notices Grant)* Who are you, and what are you doing in my house?

Grant: I'm sorry, sir. Your wife has been very generous to me. She offered me some tasty soup. Please don't sting me!

Frank: *(to Beatrice)* Really, he thinks I'm going to sting him?

Beatrice: He thinks all bees do is just see ants and sting them.

Grant: All of the stories I've heard about bees are terrifying.

Frank: Let me calm you down. Have you ever met a bee before?

Grant: No, not before you two.

Beatrice: I'll tell you what. We are going to feed you, and then Frank will fly you home. I'd like you to tell other ants about us, and let them know that we are not beasts. We are insects like everyone else. I'd also ask you to be more careful about believing all the stories you hear about other folks.

Grant: I will. Thank you very much for not stinging me.

Frank and Beatrice: *(sigh) (together)* You're welcome, Grant.

Name ______________________________

A. Reread the passage and answer the questions.

1. What does Grant believe about all bees?

____

____

____

2. Why does he believe this?

____

____

____

3. What theme does Grant's interaction with the bees show?

____

____

____

B. Work with a partner. Read the passage aloud. Pay attention to intonation. Stop after one minute. Fill out the chart.

	Words Read	–	Number of Errors	=	Words Correct Score
First Read		–		=	
Second Read		–		=	

Name ______________________________

Goldilocks Returns

Act 1, Scene 2

[Setting: *The* THREE BEARS' *kitchen. The bears are standing around their kitchen table, explaining to the* POLICE DETECTIVES *what happened.*]

MAMA BEAR: [*Worried*] As soon as we had returned from our morning stroll, we knew something wasn't right.

PAPA BEAR: [*Angry*] Each of the bowls of porridge on the kitchen table had been tasted by someone!

BABY BEAR: [*Crying*] And whoever did it ate all of my porridge!

DETECTIVE #1: [*Looks at* DETECTIVE #2] This isn't the first time we've seen this, is it, boss?

DETECTIVE #2: [*Still studying the crime scene*] No sir. Call headquarters. Tell them Goldilocks is at it again.

[*End scene.*]

Answer the questions about the text.

1. How can you tell the genre of this text is a drama?

____

____

2. How can you identify the dialogue in this text?

____

3. What do the stage directions explain?

____

____

Name ____

Read each passage. Underline the antonyms that help you figure out the meaning of each word in bold. Then write the word's meaning on the line.

1. Grant: My name is Grant. I just saw the stem to your house and climbed up. . . . But your house is lovely! (***Cowering***) Please don't sting me!

Beatrice: (*laughs*) Grant. It's nice to meet you. Stand up straight and tall. I haven't stung anyone in years, not unless they deserved it.

____

____

2. Grant: That's a relief. I have heard stories about little ants that wander away and are stung by bees. I hear bees are very **cranky**.

Beatrice: Goodness no. It takes a lot to get me irritated. I am usually very friendly.

____

____

3. Grant: All of the stories I've heard about bees are **terrifying**.

Frank: Let me calm you down. Have you ever met a bee before?

____

____

Name ______________________________

A. Read each sentence. Circle the words that include a digraph. Then underline the digraph in each word.

1. My dad will choose the patch we buy.

2. Did you snatch the bar graph I did for homework?

3. Our chef came in fifth place at the cooking contest.

4. We will have to rush to get inside the kitchen.

5. Did you touch the bottle of ketchup?

6. Did you by chance see the family photo?

B. Write the singular possessive and plural possessive forms for each noun.

Noun	Singular Possessive	Plural Possessive
1. pitcher	____________	____________
2. table	____________	____________
3. orange	____________	____________
4. theater	____________	____________
5. bus	____________	____________
6. horse	____________	____________

Name ____

A. Read the draft model. Use the questions that follow the draft to help you think about what everyday, conversational words and phrases you can add.

Draft Model

Hello, Dear Reader, my name is Theodore Baker. I have been alive almost 11 years. I am the youngest royal cake maker on the planet. Yesterday, the Queen requested that I bake her a special anniversary cake.

1. What is a more informal way for Theodore Baker to introduce himself?
2. How could Theodore Baker tell how old he is in a way that sounds more like conversation?
3. How might the Queen's request be written as dialogue?

B. Now revise the draft by adding everyday words and phrases that will make the story sound less formal and more like conversation.

____

____

____

____

____

____

____

____

____

____

Name ______________________________

Tori wrote the dialogue below using text evidence from two different sources to respond to the prompt: *Felipe has a problem. Write a dialogue that shows how Toshio helps Felipe solve the problem.*

FELIPE: All the frogs say you're a world-famous detective. You have to help me! What are you doing?

TOSHIO: Pulling out my notebook so I can take notes. How can I help?

FELIPE: I'm not a frog! *I* am the Viceroy's son! I'm under a spell!

TOSHIO: Relax. I will figure this out. Who put you under a spell, and why?

FELIPE: Vieja Sabia, but it's a long story. I know how to break the spell, though. I'm pretty sure I have to get a woman to let me eat from her *plato* and sleep in her *cama*. Then she has to kiss me at dawn.

TOSHIO: Women are funny about letting frogs eat from their *platos*. How do you know this will break the spell?

FELIPE: It worked for Ranita, didn't it?

TOSHIO: We'll talk to Vieja Sabia. Maybe she'll want to let you eat from her plate, sleep in her bed, and kiss you at dawn.

FELIPE: Yuck–no way! I'd rather stay a frog!

Reread the passage. Follow the directions below.

1. **Draw a box** around the text evidence that shows how Felipe feels about being a frog.

2. **Circle** an example of informal language that Felipe uses.

3. **Underline** the dialogue that shows how Felipe feels about eating from Vieja Sabia's plate.

4. **Write** a plural noun that Tori uses.

____

Name ______________________________

flourished	fragile	droughts	ripples
extinct	crumbled	imbalance	ecosystem

Use a word from the box to answer each question. Then use the word in a sentence.

1. What does water in a pool do when you jump in? ______________

____

2. What is another word for *delicate*? ______________

____

3. What word might describe when something broke into small pieces?

____

4. What is another word for *no longer in existence*? ______________

____

5. What might be the result if there is too much weight on one side of a boat?

____

6. What is the name of all the living and nonliving things in an area?

____

7. What is another word for *thrived*? ______________

____

8. What might cause a farm that grows corn to have problems?

____

Name ____

Read the selection. Complete the main idea and details graphic organizer.

Main Idea
Detail
Detail
Detail

Name ______________________________

Read the passage. Use the summarize strategy to make sure you understand and remember the information.

A Worm's Work

Gardener Bill works long days in the sun. He begins each day
12 digging in the dirt. He ends each day watering. But he is not alone in
27 his mission for a nice garden. His friend, the earthworm, is always
39 there to assist. The earthworm often gets a bad name as being a
52 lowly creature. Yet it has many duties and plays an important role in
65 keeping the soil rich enough to grow healthy plants.

74 **Moving and "Turning the Soil"**

79 The worms are already hard at work when Bill and his helper
91 arrive in the garden. Bill takes a shovel and digs a small hole. He sees
106 many worms moving around in the soil. This often means that the soil
119 is rich.
121 "This is a good place to plant," Bill says.
130 As the worms burrow through the soil, they create passages that
141 allow air and water to pass through. The soil and plant roots need this
155 air and water to flourish. The worms and the soil are linked.
167 Bill begins to plow the area to get ready for planting seeds. He
180 makes grooves in the dirt with his tool. This stops the soil from
193 getting too packed down.

Name ______________________________

The worms also help plow the soil. They bring down organic matter, or something that has to do with or comes from living things, from the surface. They blend it with the soil below. This turning over of the soil mixes up helpful minerals for plants to use.

Eating and Fertilization

The worms will eat almost anything organic. Grass, leaves, and animal remains are all things that the worms break down for the plants to use. By doing this, worms also keep dead matter and waste from piling up.

Bill carries the heavy bags of fertilizer into the garden. This substance contains nutrients that plants need for healthy living. He spreads the contents along the ground.

"Can you help me lift the other bag?" he asks his helper.

The worms have also been making fertilizer. As the worms eat, they leave behind droppings called castings. They contain nutrients for healthy soil. The castings also hold a lot of moisture. Dry soil can be bad for some plant roots. Moisture helps in times of little water. Last year, there was a drought in Bill's area.

"I noticed that the areas with a lot of worms did the best," Bill says.

Bill and his helper continue to watch the earthworms at work. "If the garden could talk," Bill says, "I think it would thank the worms for everything they do."

Name ____

A. Reread the passage and answer the questions.

1. What are three key details found in paragraphs 4, 6, and 7?

____

____

____

____

2. How are these details connected?

____

____

3. What is the main idea of the whole passage?

____

____

B. Work with a partner. Read the passage aloud. Pay attention to accuracy. Stop after one minute. Fill out the chart.

	Words Read	–	Number of Errors	=	Words Correct Score
First Read		–		=	
Second Read		–		=	

Name ______________________________

Dad and I See Green Worms

"Look, Dad!" I said. "These bugs are eating the lupine flowers!"

"Those are Karner Blue butterfly larvae," Dad said. "The adult butterfly lays its eggs on the lupine's stem. When the larvae hatch from their eggs, they feed only on lupine leaves until they enter the pupa stage. In recent years, the wild lupine's habitat has been shrinking, and today the Karner Blue butterfly is endangered."

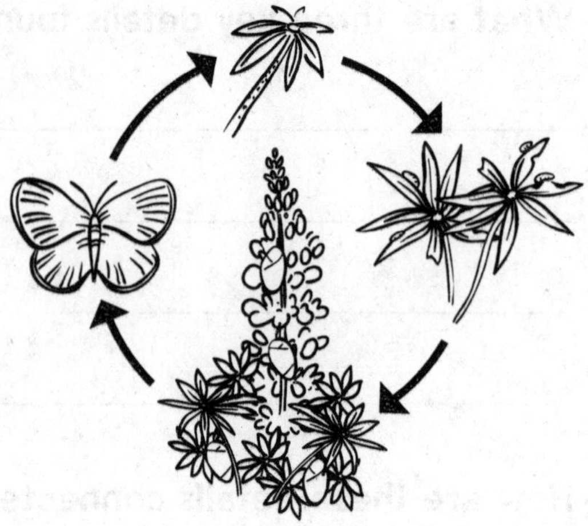

Answer the questions about the text.

1. How do you know this text is narrative nonfiction?

____

2. What text features does the text include?

____

3. What does the heading tell you? How would you change the heading to make it more effective?

____

____

____

4. What information does the flow chart give you?

____

____

Name ____

Read the sentences below. Underline the context clues that help you understand the meaning of each word in bold. Then write the word's meaning on the line.

1. But he is not alone in his **mission** for a nice garden.

   ____

2. As the worms **burrow** through the soil they create passages that allow air and water to pass through.

   ____

3. Bill begins to **plow** the area to get ready for planting seeds. He makes grooves in the dirt with his tool.

   ____

4. They bring down **organic** matter, or something that has to do with or comes from living things, from the surface.

   ____

5. This substance contains **nutrients** that plants need for healthy living.

   ____

Name ______________________________

A. Read each sentence. Circle the word that has a three-letter blend. Then write it on the line to complete the sentence.

1. The tiny ______________ came up from the ground.

   sprout blossom plant

2. I heard the owl ______________ in the night.

   cry screech squeal

3. I have a sore ______________ today.

   shoulder throat thumb

4. He will ______________ his tie before he goes on stage.

   bring clean straighten

5. The kids were ______________ in the pool.

   splashing swimming playing

B. Use *-er* or *-est* to write the correct form of the adjective.

1. wide (comparative *-er* ending) ______________
2. smart (comparative *-er* ending) ______________
3. loud (superlative *-est* ending) ______________
4. mad (comparative *-er* ending) ______________
5. cute (superlative *-est* ending) ______________
6. quick (superlative *-est* ending) ______________

Name ______________________________

A. Read the draft model. Use the questions that follow the draft to help you think about what supporting details you can add.

Draft Model

Bees and flowers need each other. The bee helps the flower. Then the flower helps the bee. Bees need the pollen that flowers have.

1. How exactly do bees and flowers benefit each other?
2. How do bees get pollen from flowers? What do bees do with the pollen?
3. How do the actions of the bees help flowers survive?
4. Without bees, how would flowers suffer? Without flowers, how would bees suffer?

B. Now revise the draft by adding supporting details that help readers understand the connection between bees and flowers.

____

____

____

____

____

____

____

____

Name ______________________________

Zoe wrote the paragraphs below using text evidence from two different sources to answer the question: *How are buffalo and owls both important parts of the food chain?*

Buffalo and owls are both important parts of the food chain because they are consumers that transfer energy between plants and animals. A food chain is made up of an energy source, producers, consumers, and decomposers. For example, in *The Buffalo Are Back,* the prairie grasses are producers because they get energy from the sun and make their own food. Buffalos are consumers because they cannot make their own food.

In "Energy in the Ecosystem," I learned that the trees and forest plants also get energy from the sun. Mice and voles are consumers because they eat the plants. Owls eat the mice and voles. Owls are higher up on the food chain because they eat other consumers.

Both buffalo and owls are important parts of the food chain because they help transfer energy in their ecosystems.

Reread the passage. Follow the directions below.

1. **Circle** the topic sentence that tells why buffalo and owls are both important parts of the food chain.

2. **Draw a box** around the text evidence that tells why buffalo are consumers.

3. **Underline** text evidence that explains why owls are higher up in the food chain.

4. **Write** one of the irregular plural nouns Zoe uses on the line.

____

Name ______________________________

pounce	prey	dribbles	poisonous
extraordinary	vibrations	camouflaged	predator

Use the context clues in each sentence to help you decide which vocabulary word fits best in the blank.

Cyril the snake was not like the other snakes in his family. He didn't like to hunt for his meals, so he wasn't much of a ______________.

"I don't care to hunt and eat mice," he told his mother. "They are not my ______________. They are my friends."

"We love to hunt mice!" said Cyril's brothers and sisters. "Cyril does not. His mouth waters at the thought of fruits and vegetables. He just ______________ and drools when he sees a good salad."

Even though Cyril had teeth that could give a ______________ bite and cause something harm, he never used them.

"Your brothers and sisters use their special coloring to be ______________ and blend in with the brown grass and leaves," said his mother. "They shake their tails back and forth to cause ______________ and make a rattling noise. This makes the mice frightened."

"I would never suddenly ______________ on any mouse, big or small," said Cyril. "They are all my friends."

Because a friendly snake was so unusual to the mice, they all thought Cyril was an ______________ friend.

Name ______________________________

Read the selection. Complete the main idea and details graphic organizer.

Main Idea
Detail
Detail
Detail

Name ______________________________

Read the passage. Use the summarize strategy to write a brief statement about the main ideas.

The Birds

Do you know why some birds have bright feathers? Have you ever
12 wondered why some birds swim better than others? Different features
22 have made life easier for birds. These are all physical adaptations
33 birds have made in order to survive.

40 **The Web**

42 Many birds that live near water spend a lot of their time in the
56 water. These birds, called waterfowl, have webbed feet. Why is this
67 helpful? Webbed feet are like the paddles on a boat, which help the
80 waterfowl move through the water faster.

86 **Big Mouth**

88 The shape of a bird's beak is useful for specific tasks. The
100 spoonbill has a spoon-shaped beak. Why a spoon shape? This bird
111 spends a lot of time in the water. The spoon shape helps the bird stir
126 the water. The stirring causes little whirlpools. Small fish and insects
137 get pulled into the whirlpools, making it easy for the bird to snap up
151 a meal.

153 **Light as a Feather**

157 It is not uncommon to see birds with pretty feathers. Feathers are
169 for more than looking good, though. For the penguin, they do two
181 things. The outer part of the feather is waterproof. This keeps the
193 penguin dry. The inner part of the feather, called the down, traps
205 air that keeps it warm. This is important since penguins don't fly.
217 Instead, they swim in freezing water. Without waterproof feathers,
226 they would be at a disadvantage.

Name ____

True Colors

The toucan's beak can be many colors.

Ingram Publishing/SuperStock

Bright colors help some birds stand out. The golden pheasant has red, green, and gold feathers. The toucan's large beak can be many colors at once. Bright colors help these two birds get noticed. This attention helps them find a mate.

There are some birds who are just the opposite. They do not want to be seen at all! The potoo has coloring that makes it look just like part of a tree. This camouflage helps the potoo avoid unwanted attention.

Voices Carry

Birds have different ways of talking. They have calls to find a mate, warn other birds, and to say "I live here!"

The killdeer has a special reason for one of its calls. This bird builds its nest on the ground. This can be unsafe. When a predator is too close to the nest, the killdeer gives a loud call. The bird hops around and pretends to be injured. This loud call and unusual act distract the predator. The predator will now go after the injured bird rather than look for the nest. When the predator gets too close the bird flies to safety, then to its nest. The killdeer's call and act help protect its nest.

The club-winged manakin has an interesting call, too. This bird uses its wings to "talk." It moves its feathers back and forth over one another. It can sound like a violin.

Birds have to adapt to their environments. Different environments require different features. Whether it's a certain way of moving, eating, or talking, various adaptations help birds to survive.

Name ____

A. Reread the passage and answer the questions.

1. What is the main idea in the third paragraph?

____

____

2. What are the key details in the fourth paragraph?

____

____

____

3. How are these details connected?

____

____

B. Work with a partner. Read the passage aloud. Pay attention to rate. Stop after one minute. Fill out the chart.

	Words Read	–	Number of Errors	=	Words Correct Score
First Read		–		=	
Second Read		–		=	

Name ______________________________

Giraffes' Adaptations

Where giraffes live there are few kinds of plants for animals to eat. So giraffes' bodies have adapted to eat the plants that are available. Giraffes mainly eat the leaves of the acacia tree. The acacia tree's branches are hard and thorny, but the giraffe's long, flexible tongue allows it to reach around the thorns and pluck the leaves. Even if a thorny branch does get into a giraffe's mouth, it has thick saliva that coats the thorns and protects its mouth from cuts.

fabio lotti/Alamy Stock Photo

The giraffe's flexible tongue reaches between the thorns to remove the leaves.

Answer the questions about the text.

1. How do you know this text is expository text?

____

____

2. What text features does the text include?

____

3. What is the heading? Give an example of the topic it introduces.

____

____

4. How do the caption and photo help you understand the text better?

____

____

Name ______________________________

Read each sentence below. Then answer each question about the word in bold.

1. The prefix *un-* means "not." What does **uncommon** mean in the following sentence? "It is not **uncommon** to see birds with pretty feathers."

____

2. What does **unwanted** mean in the following sentence? "This camouflage helps the potoo avoid **unwanted** attention."

____

3. What does **unusual** mean in the following sentence? "This loud call and **unusual** act distract the predator."

____

4. The prefix *dis-* means "opposite or lack of." What does **disadvantage** mean in the following sentence? "Without waterproof feathers, they would be at a **disadvantage**."

____

5. The prefix *re-* means "again." What does **reproduce** mean in the following sentence? "This attention helps them find a mate and **reproduce**."

____

Name ______________________________

A. Circle the word with the /är/ or /ôr/ sound to complete each sentence. The /är/ sound is found in the word *star*. The /ôr/ sound is found in the word *fort*.

1. The boys saw a ______________ on the roof of the house.

   hawk stork owl

2. The deck will ______________ because of all the rain.

   warp break bend

3. I liked the new ______________ that was in the bedroom.

   light chair carpet

4. It is always helpful to have ______________ friends.

   kind smart many

5. They wanted to have the party in the ______________.

   backyard evening basement

B. The suffix *-ful* means "full of" or "having." The suffix *-less* means "without." Add the suffix to each word on the first line. Then write the meaning of each word on the second line.

1. pity + less = ______________ ______________

2. wonder + ful = ______________ ______________

3. sense + less = ______________ ______________

4. care + ful = ______________ ______________

5. doubt + ful ______________ ______________

6. penny + less = ______________ ______________

Name ______________________________

A. Read the draft model. Use the questions that follow the draft to help you think about what logical order to use to present details.

Draft Model

A giraffe has spots on its coat. Giraffes are tall animals from Africa. They are between 14 and 19 feet tall.

1. How could ideas be rearranged to help readers better understand what the text is about?
2. What other animals are giraffes related to?
3. What animals are giraffes taller than?
4. What other animal has spots on its coat?

B. Now revise the draft by rearranging ideas and presenting them in a logical order to help readers better understand giraffes.

____

____

____

____

____

____

____

____

____

Name ______________________________

Grant wrote the paragraphs below using text evidence from two different sources to respond to the prompt: ***Compare Nic Bishop's explanation of how spiders make silk to the Anansi story's explanation.***

How spiders make silk is described very differently in *Spiders* and "Anansi and the Birds." In *Spiders,* Nic Bishop presents facts about spiders' bodies and the silk they make. However, "Anansi and the Birds" does not have facts. Instead, it tells a story to explain how spiders make silk.

Nic Bishop explains that spiders use the spinnerets on their abdomens to shoot out threads of silk. In "Anansi and the Birds," Anansi falls over a cliff and an owl tells him to push in his belly. Anansi does this and suddenly threads of silk shoot out behind him. In *Spiders,* there are important facts about real spiders, but in "Anansi and the Birds," Anansi's silk is used to teach a lesson. Anansi is not a real spider, but he uses his silk the same way real spiders do.

Reread the passage. Follow the directions below.

1. **Underline** the topic sentence of Grant's response.

2. **Draw a box** around the text evidence that shows what Owl told Anansi.

3. **Circle** an example of a transition word in Grant's response.

4. **Write** the singular possessive noun Grant uses on the line below.

____

Name ______________________________

brittle   creative   descriptive   outstretched

Finish each sentence using the vocabulary word provided.

1. **(creative)** The artist is respected ______________________________

______________________________.

2. **(outstretched)** Before she made the amazing catch, ______________________________

______________________________.

3. **(descriptive)** I really like the author's writing because ______________________________

______________________________.

4. **(brittle)** The old newspaper I found in the attic ______________________________

______________________________.

Name ____

Read the selection. Complete the point of view graphic organizer.

Details

↓

Point of View

Name ____

Read the poem. Check your understanding as you read by asking yourself how the speaker thinks and feels.

Deer

The headlights turn their dark eyes
6 green.
7 We see them sitting under trees
13 at night, in my yard, like a photo of
22 a family.

24 Then they dart away, their tails held
31 high,
32 six white arrows point at the sky.
39 We don't even get to say good-bye.

47 Into the night they disappear,
52 and though they move as quick as spears
60 a little later they'll be back here.

67 Our lights go off, we're warm inside,
74 they come out then, from where they hide.
82 Their secret place is a point of pride.

90 Calm as ponds, they never fight,
96 they stand and leave when the sky gets bright.
105 But the question never sat quite right—

112 where do they go when it gets light?

Name ____

A. Reread the passage and answer the questions.

1. What point of view is the poem told from?

____

____

2. How do you know which point of view it is told from?

____

____

3. What does the speaker think about the deer?

____

____

B. Work with a partner. Read the passage aloud. Pay attention to expression and phrasing. Stop after one minute. Fill out the chart.

	Words Read	–	Number of Errors	=	Words Correct Score
First Read		–		=	
Second Read		–		=	

Name ______________________________

The Nautilus

The strangest creature in the sea?
Some say the eight-legged octopus.
The oddest always seemed to me
To be the baffling nautilus.

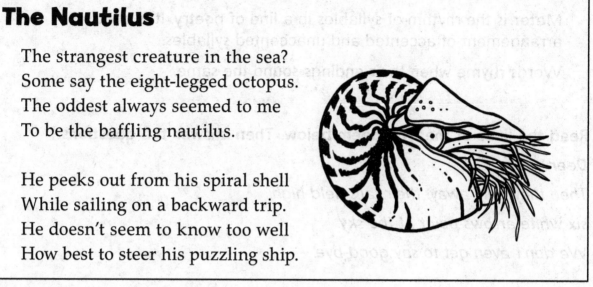

He peeks out from his spiral shell
While sailing on a backward trip.
He doesn't seem to know too well
How best to steer his puzzling ship.

Answer the questions about the text.

1. What makes this poem a lyric poem?

____

2. What is the rhyme scheme of this poem?

____

3. What does the poet think about the nautilus?

____

____

Name ____

Meter is the rhythm of syllables in a line of poetry. It is created by the arrangement of accented and unaccented syllables.

Words **rhyme** when their endings sound the same.

Read the lines of the lyric poem below. Then answer the questions.

Deer

Then they dart away, their tails held high,
six white arrows point at the sky.
We don't even get to say good-bye.

Into the night they disappear,
and though they move as quick as spears
a little later they'll be back here.

1. **Find two examples of rhyme in the poem. Write them below.**

____

2. **What kind of meter appears in the poem?**

____

3. **How do the meter and rhyme affect the poem?**

____

____

4. **Write another stanza for this poem that includes meter and rhyme.**

____

____

____

Name ______________________________

Read each passage. Underline the simile or metaphor in the sentence. Then write the two things that are being compared on the lines.

1. We see them sitting under trees
at night, in my yard, like a photo of a family.

____

____

2. Then they dart away, their tails held high,
six white arrows point at the sky.

____

____

3. Into the night they disappear,
and though they move as quick as spears
a little later they'll be back here.

____

____

Name ______________________________

A. Read each sentence. Circle the word that has a suffix. Write the base word and the suffix on the lines.

1. We had a great time listening to the classical music.

 Base Word: __________ **Suffix:** _______

2. I could see the teacher walking up the steep stairs.

 Base Word: __________ **Suffix:** _______

3. My dad thinks that your answer is acceptable.

 Base Word: __________ **Suffix:** _______

4. A quality education is something that will always help you.

 Base Word: __________ **Suffix:** _______

5. There is a visitor waiting for you downstairs.

 Base Word: __________ **Suffix:** _______

B. Read each word pair. Write the contraction on the line.

1. was not ____________
2. they are ____________
3. he will ____________
4. should not ____________
5. we would ____________
6. were not ____________
7. has not ____________
8. they will ____________

Name ____

A. Read the draft model. Use the questions that follow the draft to add precise language that will help the reader create a picture in his or her mind.

Draft Model

We have a hamster named Teddy. He is small. We keep Teddy in a cage with a water bottle and a wheel. Teddy likes to run in his wheel for hours at a time.

1. What does Teddy look like? How small is he?

2. How long has the writer had this pet?

3. What words can be used to better describe Teddy's cage?

4. What strong verbs or descriptive adjectives can be added to describe what Teddy is like and how the writer feels about the pet?

B. Now revise the draft by adding precise language to help the reader create a picture in his or her mind.

____

____

____

____

____

____

____

____

Name ______________________________

Katia wrote the poem below using text evidence from different poems to respond to the prompt: *Write a lyric poem about an animal that is a predator. Use rhyme and a simile.*

The Lion

On the African plains,
as the day drifts into night
Lion sniffs and raises her head.

Her eyes glow as yellow
as the full moon's light.
A herd of antelope pauses

to graze, unaware
of the stalking predator
and her hungry stare.

Reread the poem. Follow the directions below.

1. **Circle** an example of a simile.
2. **Draw a box** around words that rhyme.
3. **Underline** an example of precise language.
4. **Write** the line of the poem that is an example of combining sentences.

____

____

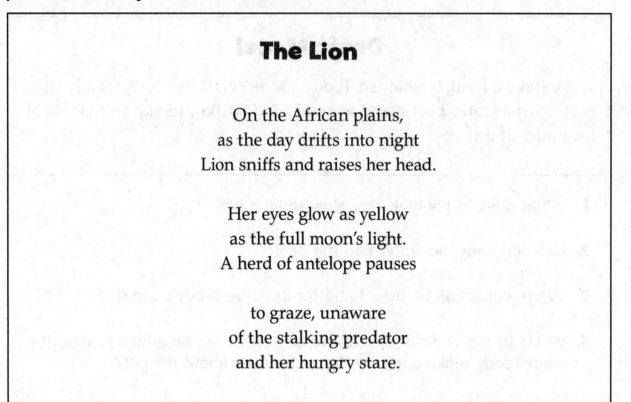

Name ______________________

acquaintance	complementary	logical	scrounging
cautiously	jumble	scornfully	trustworthy

Use a word from the box to answer each question. Then use the word in a sentence.

1. What were the mice doing when they were looking on the ground for food?

____

2. Which word could you use to describe a mess? ______________________

____

3. What do you call a person you know? ______________________

____

4. How was the judge acting when she told the politician he had broken the law?

____

5. What is another word for *carefully*? ______________________

____

6. How would you describe someone you can rely on? ______________________

____

7. Which word would describe someone who is very sensible? ______________________

____

8. What is another word for *making whole*? ______________________

____

Name ______________________________

Read the selection. Complete the point of view graphic organizer.

Details

↓

Point of View

Name ______________________________

Read the passage. Use the visualize strategy to help you understand the fantasy story.

The Oak Tree and the Tiny Bird

Far out in the country, in the middle of a grassy field, there lived
14 a beautiful oak tree. The oak tree loved her home, there in the field.
28 She loved the feel of squirrels jumping from limb to limb. She loved
41 watching the sun rise every morning and dip below the horizon
52 each night. She liked the feeling of wind in her branches. During
64 rainstorms, she enjoyed feeling the water run down her trunk.
74 One morning, the tree heard a tiny bird chirping sadly in her
86 branches. The tree looked and saw a baby bluebird there, trembling.
97 He was alone in a nest of twigs and feathers. The baby bird was
111 shaking with fright.
114 "What is the matter, little bird?" asked the tree.
123 The tiny bird jumped. He looked surprised, startled by the tree's
134 question. The bird choked back a few tears before saying, "It's my
146 mother. She left the nest two nights ago to go get me some food, and
161 she still hasn't come back."
166 The tree had seen this happen before. Sometimes mama birds leave
177 their nest to get food and run into danger. And sometimes, they stay
190 away longer than they planned.
195 "Well, your mother may be gone, but you still have me," said the
208 tree. "First things first. Let's get some food in that belly."
219 The oak tree saw some squirrels scrounging around on the ground.
230 They were running all over, picking up food.
238 "You there, squirrel," whispered the tree. "Will you share some of
249 your nuts and berries with this good little bluebird?"

Name ______________________________

"Sure!" said the squirrel. He dashed into his home in the tree. He reappeared just as fast with his paws full of food. The squirrel ran again to the bird's nest and tossed in nuts and berries. The tiny bird ate everything up and felt much better.

"You must be thirsty," said the tree. The tree carefully shook her limbs. She cautiously bent her branches, and morning dew from her leaves trickled down to the bird's open mouth.

With the help of the squirrels and occasionally other animals, the oak tree kept the tiny bird fed and watered. Every once in a while, an owl helped out. Sometimes a rainstorm passed over the grassy field, and the tree would gently put her limbs around the tiny bird to protect him from the wind and rain.

This went on for weeks. Slowly but surely, the tiny bird began to grow.

One day, the tree went to check on the tiny bluebird, but the bird was not in his nest. The tree searched all over her limbs and trunk, and even the ground, but she could not see the tiny bird anywhere. "What could have happened?" thought the tree. Just then, with a flutter of wings, the bluebird, which the tree had loved and cared for all these weeks, flew and landed among the branches. He had a mouthful of nice, juicy worms.

"Why, you're all grown up," exclaimed the tree. "And you can fly!"

"All thanks to you," replied the not-so-tiny bluebird with a smile.

Name ____

A. Reread the passage and answer the questions.

1. What two pronouns are used in the first paragraph? Which character do the pronouns refer to?

____

____

2. Does the narrator take part in the events of the story? Explain. What point of view is the story told from?

____

____

3. What is the narrator's point of view about animals and nature? Give evidence or details from the story.

____

____

____

B. Work with a partner. Read the passage aloud. Pay attention to expression. Stop after one minute. Fill out the chart.

	Words Read	–	Number of Errors	=	Words Correct Score
First Read		–		=	
Second Read		–		=	

Name ______________________________

A Perfect Room

"What do you think of the room we made for you?" the gooey creatures asked their new robot friend. "Most of the rooms here are made out of ooze and slime, but we thought you might like something different."

The robot looked around. The floor was made of bright, gleaming metal. The furniture had perfectly straight edges. The closets' contents were all clearly labeled. "I love it!" she beeped.

Answer the questions about the text.

1. What is the genre of this text?

____

2. How does the illustration help you to identify the genre?

____

____

3. Describe one of the characters in the text. Could the character you chose exist in real life?

____

____

4. Describe the setting of the text. Could the setting exist in real life?

____

____

Name ____

Read each passage. Underline the context clues that help you figure out the meaning of each word in bold. Then write the word's meaning on the line.

1. The tree looked and saw a baby bluebird there, **trembling**. He was alone in a nest of twigs and feathers. The baby bird was shaking with fright.

____

2. The tiny bird jumped. He looked surprised, **startled** by the tree's question.

____

3. "Sure!" said the squirrel. He **dashed** into his home in the tree. He reappeared just as fast with his paws full of food. The squirrel ran again to the bird's nest and tossed in nuts and berries.

____

4. The tree carefully shook her limbs. She **cautiously** bent her branches, and morning dew from her leaves trickled down to the bird's open mouth.

____

5. With the help of the squirrels and **occasionally** other animals, the oak tree kept the tiny bird fed and watered. Every once in a while, an owl helped out.

____

Name ______________________________

A. To complete each sentence, circle the word that has the /ûr/ sound found in *shirt*. Then write the word on the line.

1. I watched the acrobat ____________ the ribbon in the air.

   hold roll twirl

2. We had to go home because my mom forgot her ____________.

   ring purse form

3. The ____________ at the zoo scared my little sister.

   lion tiger shark

4. After the game, my shirt was ____________.

   dirty ripped torn

5. The brave woman pulled a ____________ from the basket.

   snake flame serpent

B. Read the words in the box. Sort them according to the number of closed syllables.

cargo	pillow	pencil	raven	garlic	panda

Words with One Closed Syllable	Words with Two Closed Syllables
1.	4.
2.	5.
3.	6.

Name ______________________________

A. Read the draft model. Use the questions that follow the draft to help you think about what transitions you can add.

Draft Model

Liz was nervous about her first day at the underwater school. She fidgeted inside her airtight pod. Her teacher, a lobster, greeted her. She made friends with a fish. She had a good day.

1. What transition words or phrases might show a cause-and-effect relationship between Liz's nervousness and her fidgeting?
2. What transition words or phrases might help connect the ideas in the rest of the passage?
3. What transition words or phrases could be added to make clear the order of events?

B. Now revise the draft by adding transition words and phrases to help tell the order of events and to connect ideas.

____

____

____

____

____

____

____

____

Name ____

Shaun wrote the letter below using text evidence from two different sources to respond to the prompt: ***Write a letter to Tucker Mouse from Chenoo's granddaughter thanking Tucker for his help in Times Square.***

Dear Tucker,

It was great to meet you. I am not sure what would have happened if you hadn't helped me in the Times Square subway station.

I told my brothers all about our meeting in Times Square. What a busy, loud subway station! I was so frightened that I was trembling. I can't believe that you were able to hear me asking strangers for directions. At first, I didn't see you in your drain pipe. Then, I heard you calling out to me. Next, I looked down and there you were! Thank you for offering me a piece of liverwurst. It was the first time I ever tried it and it's much better than the hare and goose that I usually eat.

I would like to invite you to visit us up north so I can prepare a big feast for you. My grandfather and brothers would like to meet you and hear about living in Times Square.

Your friend,
Chenoo's Granddaughter

Reread the passage. Follow the directions below.

1. **Circle** two examples of precise words that describe how Chenoo's granddaughter felt in the Times Square subway station.

2. **Underline** a time-order word that shows sequence of events.

3. **Draw a box** around a pronoun that shows the letter has a first-person narrator.

4. **Write** one of the action verbs that Shaun uses on the line.

____

Name ____________________

mature	assigned	residents	gingerly
selective	scattered	generosity	organizations

Use the context clues in each sentence to help you decide which vocabulary word fits best in the blank.

The students of the two volunteer ______________ were excited to be going on a trip. Due to all their hard work and the ______________ they showed by helping others, the students were rewarded with a trip to an apple orchard.

After about an hour drive, the students arrived at their destination. They were welcomed by a few of the ______________ who lived at the orchard all year long. The manager explained how they would help gather apples, which the students planned to give to those in need.

"I'm really excited to have you here," the manager said. "I have ______________ each of you to a part of the orchard. This way you won't be picking apples from the same trees. I need you to be very ______________ and only pick apples that are ______________ and ripe."

After some more instructions, the students were ______________ to different parts of the orchard. The students had a great time as they ______________ climbed ladders in order to pick the best apples.

Name ______________________________

Read the selection. Complete the point of view graphic organizer.

Details

↓

Point of View

Name ____

Read the passage. Use the visualize strategy to make sure you understand what you read.

How Vera Helped

"Excuse me. Are you going to drink that extra juice box?"
11 Brad turned around to see who was speaking to him. It was Vera.
24 Not again, Brad thought. "Um, I guess not. Here you go." Brad
36 handed Vera the second apple juice his mother always packed. She put
48 it in the reusable shopping bag she was carrying.
57 "Thank you so much," she said, smiling, then marched to the next
69 table.
70 Brad rotated back to his friends who sat with him at his lunch table,
84 rolled his eyes, and said, "She's so weird, always walking from table
96 to table, asking people for their food. Do you think she eats it all?"
110 His friends laughed. They wondered the same thing.
118 Vera had been collecting food since the beginning of the school
129 year. The first time she had asked Brad for his leftover food had been
143 back in September. Brad had been in the middle of deciding whether
155 to eat his extra apple, when Vera had asked him if she could have it.
170 He had been so surprised by her request, that he had just handed it to
185 her. It was November now, and Brad was curious about what happened
197 to all those juice boxes and food he gave away.
207 "Do you guys want to find out where all that food goes?" Brad
220 asked his friends. They didn't seem very interested. But it was a
232 Friday afternoon, and there wasn't any homework to do. So he decided
244 to go alone. He'd follow Vera after school and see what happened.

Name ____

After the last bell rang, Brad said good-bye to his friends. Then he waited around until he saw Vera leave. Her shopping bag was bulging. The edges of boxes were pushing out against the bag. Brad didn't know where she lived, so he stuck close behind.

When Vera walked into her house, Brad said out loud, "Wow, maybe she does eat it all. Maybe her family needs the food." He felt unsure as he said it. Her family had a beautiful house with a trimmed yard. But he was truly confused. He didn't know what to make of what he was seeing.

Brad was getting ready to go home when Vera came out of her house. She was carrying a small brown cardboard box. In it, Brad recognized all of the extra food she had collected at lunch!

Vera walked down her block to a house that was four doors down, as Brad quietly followed. She knocked on the front door. A moment later, an elderly man opened the door. Brad couldn't hear what the older man said to Vera, but they both smiled. He took the box from her, went back inside, and closed the door.

As Vera turned onto the sidewalk to walk back to her house, Brad was in front of her. "Hi, Brad," Vera said, looking a little puzzled. "What are you doing here?"

Brad said, "I wanted to know what you did with all that food! You just collect what other kids don't want. That is kind of odd."

Vera explained that her family was friendly with some of the older people in her neighborhood, and she collected the food to bring to them. "Sometimes it is hard for them to leave their homes," she explained.

"Okay, that's not odd. That's a great idea," Brad said. "What can I do to help?"

Name ____

A. Reread the passage and answer the questions.

1. What kind of narrator does the story use? How do you know?

____

____

____

2. What details at the end of the story help you figure out the narrator's point of view?

____

____

____

3. What is the narrator's point of view?

____

____

B. Work with a partner. Read the passage aloud. Pay attention to expression. Stop after one minute. Fill out the chart.

	Words Read	–	Number of Errors	=	Words Correct Score
First Read		–		=	
Second Read		–		=	

Name ______________________________

The Bag Parade

Jane was receiving the Citizenship Award during her eighth-grade graduation. As she stood on the stage with the other award winners, she thought about the actions she took that led her to this award.

Four years ago, Jane and her friends were walking home from school. They saw litter all over the sidewalk. Her friend Alex said, "We need to do something. What if we organize a Garbage Bag Parade?" Jane didn't know what she meant. Alex explained that they could invite neighbors to help clean up the street next Saturday. After they filled the bags, they could take them to the dumpsters at the community center. It would be like a parade!

Jane smiled and listened to the end of the principal's introduction. Then she walked across the stage to accept the award.

Answer the questions about the text.

1. How do you know this text is realistic fiction?

____

____

2. How do you know that there is a flashback in this text?

____

____

3. How do you recognize dialogue in the text?

____

4. Identify two ways that the characters in the text seem like real people.

____

____

Name ____

Read the following sentences from the passage. Underline the context clues that help you figure out the meaning of each word in bold. Write a short definition of the word on the line. Then use the word correctly in a sentence.

1. Vera had been collecting food since the beginning of the school year. . . . It was November now, and Brad was **curious** about what happened to all those juice boxes and food he gave away.

____

____

2. Her shopping bag was **bulging**. The edges of boxes were pushing out against the bag.

____

____

3. When Vera walked into her house, Brad said out loud, "Wow, maybe she does eat it all. Maybe her family needs the food." He felt unsure as he said it. Her family had a beautiful house with a trimmed yard. But he was truly **confused**. He didn't know what to make of what he was seeing.

____

____

4. She knocked on the front door. A moment later, an **elderly** man opened the door. Brad couldn't hear what the older man said to Vera, but they both smiled.

____

____

Name ______________________________

A. Read each sentence. Circle the words that have silent letters.

1. I watched the newborn lambs wriggle free from their mother.

2. We asked the plumber to be careful while using the old wrench.

3. She knew the group would look away from the ghastly sight.

4. I was doubtful that he would give us a truthful answer.

5. The honest worker had to resign when he made too many mistakes.

B. Read each word. Circle the open syllables. Underline the closed syllables. Then check the correct box.

	Only Open Syllables	Only Closed Syllables	Both Open Syllables and Closed Syllables
1. spoken	☐	☐	☐
2. planet	☐	☐	☐
3. label	☐	☐	☐
4. banjo	☐	☐	☐
5. refund	☐	☐	☐
6. photo	☐	☐	☐

Name ______________________________

A. Read the draft model. Use the questions that follow the draft to help you think about what strong words you can add.

Draft Model

Lawrence saw the ship. He steered his canoe toward the ship. As he got closer, he could hear the cries for help. Lawrence saw two people on the ship.

1. What strong words would tell when and how Lawrence first saw the ship?
2. What specific verbs or concrete details would show how Lawrence steered the canoe?
3. What strong descriptive words would give readers a clearer picture of the passengers and the ship?

B. Now revise the draft by adding strong words to make the story about the ship clearer and more interesting to read.

____

____

____

____

____

____

____

____

Name ______________________________

Ava wrote the paragraphs below using text evidence from two different sources to respond to the prompt: *Write a scene between Marilia in* Aguinaldo *and Katie Stagliano in* "Partaking in Public Service." *Use descriptive details and dialogue to show how the girls help their communities.*

Katie's face appeared on Marilia's computer screen. "Hi!" Marilia exclaimed. "What are you growing in your garden?"

Katie held a bunch of carrots up to the screen. Dirt clung to their damp orange tips. "I just pulled these carrots for the food bank," Katie said.

Marilia was thinking about the words she would use to describe the carrots to Elenita: *as thin and pointed as pencils.*

"Hey, did I tell you?" Katie continued. "Some of the cabbages weigh forty pounds. That's enough to feed almost 300 people!"

Marilia held up the garden collage she had made for Elenita. Marilia had glued soft cotton balls in the sky. Elenita might not be able to see the white, wispy clouds, but she'd be able to feel them.

Katie smiled. "Marilia, that's beautiful. Why don't you plant a garden? Then you could bring Elenita fresh vegetables when you visit."

Marilia clapped her hands. "I'll do it! And I can ask you for advice."

Reread the passage. Follow the directions below.

1. **Circle** a sensory detail that Ava includes in her narrative.

2. **Draw a box around** an example of dialogue that shows that Katie contributes to the food bank.

3. **Underline** an inference that Ava makes about what Marilia would say.

4. **Write** one of the progressive verb tenses that Ava uses on the line.

____

Name ____

mistreated	encouragement	qualified	boycott
fulfill	registered	protest	injustice

Finish each sentence using the vocabulary word provided.

1. **(protest)** We didn't want them to shut the library down ______________________ ____.

2. **(registered)** The new baseball league starts next week ______________________ ____.

3. **(fulfill)** My sister picked me up from school ______________________ ____.

4. **(qualified)** To have a good president of our school ______________________ ____.

5. **(boycott)** When my mother was younger, ______________________ ____.

6. **(mistreated)** When we got blamed for ______________________ ____.

7. **(encouragement)** My brother was having trouble with his painting ______________________ ____.

8. **(injustice)** The police officer told us ______________________ ____.

Name ____

Read the selection. Complete the author's point of view graphic organizer.

Details

↓

Author's Point of View

Name ______________________________

Read the passage. Use the reread strategy to help you understand and remember information.

A Child's Fight for Rights

At age 12, Craig Kielburger of Ontario, Canada, read a terrible
11 news story that changed his life. He read about Iqbal Masik. Iqbal
23 was a boy from Pakistan who was forced to work in a rug factory.
37 Craig read that children were taken from their homes. They were put
49 to work at very young ages. Craig was free. The thought of being
62 captive shocked him.

65 **Iqbal's Story**

67 Iqbal was the same age as Craig. He had been working constant
79 12-hour days since age four. Non-stop working kept Iqbal from going
90 to school. He was not treated well and lived behind large fences and
103 walls.

104 Iqbal was later set free by police. He tried to make his story known
118 and spoke to the press.

123 **Free the Children**

126 Craig was moved by Iqbal's story. It caused him and his friends
138 to write requests and reach out to world leaders to raise money for a
152 wonderful cause.

154 In 1996, Craig founded Free the Children. It was started as a group
167 of young people who wanted to stop the use of child labor around the
181 world.

Name ______________________________

Craig Kielburger and Free the Children

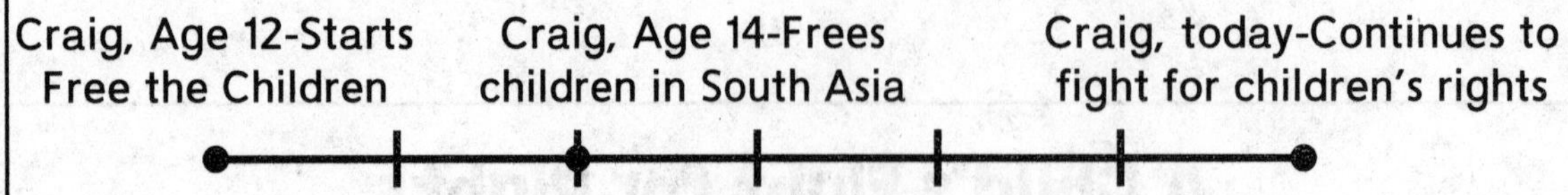
Craig, Age 12-Starts Free the Children
Craig, Age 14-Frees children in South Asia
Craig, today-Continues to fight for children's rights

Many people were not aware that children were being forced to work in factories. Free the Children helped make sure that Canada checked the rugs that were brought into the country. The rugs that were not made by children were labeled.

When Craig was 14, he went with police in South Asia to search for children who were being forced to work. The children were returned to their parents. Craig spoke with the parents and learned the families' stories.

Conflict and Results

Some people disagreed with Craig. They didn't agree with him because they thought he was too young. They didn't like that he was talking about these things.

That didn't stop Craig's group though. After two years, the group used the money they had raised to pay for a center in Pakistan. The center provided shelter and education for children who had escaped capture.

Free the Children still thrives today. It grows because countries like the United States and Germany have learned of Craig's mission. They have taken action. Children raise money with car washes and bake sales.

Craig has helped to build over 100 schools and centers for children in need. With his help and that of other interested people, Craig's group can complete its goal of fighting for children's rights—a very worthy cause.

Name ____________________

A. Reread the passage and answer the questions.

1. What are two details from paragraphs 1 and 4 that tell us the author's point of view?

____

____

2. How are the two details similar?

____

____

3. What is the author's point of view in the passage? Give evidence or reasons from the passage.

____

____

____

B. Work with a partner. Read the passage aloud. Pay attention to accuracy. Stop after one minute. Fill out the chart.

	Words Read	–	Number of Errors	=	Words Correct Score
First Read		–		=	
Second Read		–		=	

Name ____

Talia Leman and Randomkid.org

In 2005, Hurricane Katrina hit the Gulf Coast of the United States hard. Ten-year-old Talia Leman helped raise over $10 million to help the victims.

Leman then founded the Web site RandomKid.org. It helps a variety of causes across the globe and has won awards and widespread recognition. Over 12 million young people in 20 countries have joined its effort.

In 2011, Leman won the National Jefferson Award for global change. It was her reward for all of her public service.

Important Events in Talia Leman's Life

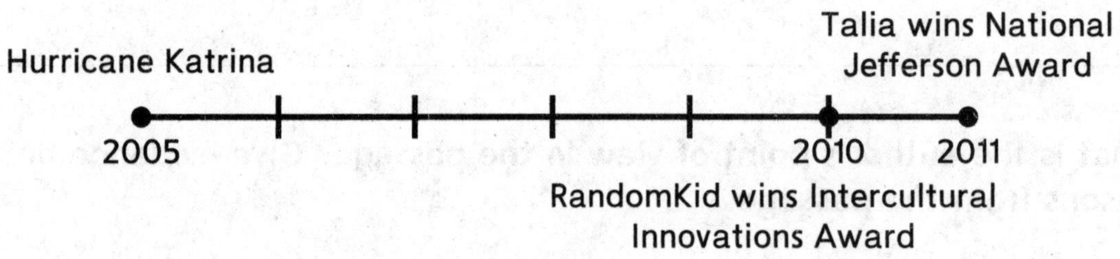

Answer the questions about the text.

1. How do you know this text is a biography?

____

2. What is one text feature included in this text?

____

3. How does the time line help you understand the text better?

____

____

4. How can you tell that the events in the text are in the order that they happened?

____

Name ____

Read the sentences below. Underline the word in the second sentence that is a synonym or an antonym of the word in bold. Then write the best definition of the word you underlined on the line.

1. Craig was **free**. The thought of being captive shocked him.

____

2. He had been working **constant** 12-hour days since age four. Non-stop working kept Iqbal from going to school.

____

3. Craig was **moved** by Iqbal's story. It caused him and his friends to write requests and reach out to world leaders to raise money for a wonderful cause.

____

4. In 1996, Craig **founded** Free the Children. It was started as a group of young people who wanted to stop the use of child labor around the world.

____

5. Some people **disagreed** with Craig. They didn't agree with him because they thought he was too young.

____

Name ______________________________

A. Read each sentence. Circle the word with the soft *c* or soft *g* to complete the sentence. Then write the word on the line.

1. The performers were a big hit at the ______________.

   game carnival circus

2. The kids were ______________ their plan to stay up late would work.

   certain positive sure

3. ______________ are a great source of vitamins.

   Grapes Oranges Mangoes

4. The wet ______________ fell on the kitchen floor.

   sponge glue grease

5. Did you see the ______________ car drive down the street?

   silver colorful police

B. Read each sentence. Circle the word with the final VCe pattern. Then write that final *e* syllable on the line.

Final *e* Syllable

1. Did you complete your homework yet? ______________
2. The ballet dancer is very agile. ______________
3. The hikers want to escape the jungle. ______________
4. Does it excite you to play sports? ______________
5. Which reptile do you want to see first? ______________
6. You must include all of your work. ______________

Name ______________________________

A. Read the draft model. Use the questions that follow the draft to help you think about what reasons and evidence you can add.

Draft Model

Miss Cardenas made a big difference in our community. She started a nursing school five years ago. There was a shortage of skilled nurses in our town before the school opened.

1. What efforts did Miss Cardenas make to start the nursing school?
2. What concrete details would describe the problem with the nurse shortage?
3. What reasons and evidence would show how the school helped end the shortage?
4. What examples would show how things got better?

B. Now revise the draft by adding reasons and evidence that will help convince readers to agree with the writer's opinion.

____

____

____

____

____

____

____

____

Name ______________________________

Sebastian wrote the paragraphs below using text evidence from two different sources to answer the question: *Can one person's actions make the world a better place?*

I think that one person can make the world a better place. How you act affects the people you deal with every day. If you respect people's rights, you make life better for everyone. You help change society. Some people, like Westley in *Delivering Justice,* may be natural leaders who organize large movements to make society better. He organized a large boycott for civil rights. I think even one person, or only a few people, can help change the world. The Davis children did this. In "Keeping Freedom in the Family," the author describes how they had their own boycott to fight for civil rights.

I think everyone can act to support equal rights, just like Westley and the Davis children. Each person can do something helpful. A person might join a large protest. Or a person might act alone to help in a small way. Small actions may lead to large actions, and large actions may result in real change. Everyone's actions are important and can help change the world.

Reread the passage. Follow the directions below.

1. **Circle** a sentence that tells you how Sebastian feels about small actions.

2. **Underline** a sentence that shows Sebastian's opinion about the topic.

3. **Draw a box around** an example of the text evidence Sebastian uses to support his opinion.

4. **Write** one sentence from the text that uses a main verb and a helping verb. Underline the main verb and the helping verb.

____

Name ______________________________

haste	divided	shattered	tension
opposed	perish	proclamation	address

Use a word from the box to answer each question. Then use the word in a sentence.

1. What word might be used to describe mental strain? ____________

____

2. What is an official public announcement? ____________

____

3. If something is in two separate pieces, what is it? ____________

____

4. What is another word for *quickness*? ____________

____

5. What word might describe something broken in many pieces?

____

6. If you do not take care of a plant, what might it do? ____________

____

7. What is another word for *against*? ____________

____

8. What might a politician give to a crowd of people? ____________

____

Name ______________________________

Read the selection. Complete the author's point of view graphic organizer.

Details

↓

Author's Point of View

Name ____

Read the passage. Use the reread strategy to make sure you understand the text.

A True Declaration

Do you like to write? What if you wrote words that helped form
13 laws? This is what Thomas Jefferson did. He was the third president
25 of the United States, but he might be best known for writing the
38 Declaration of Independence.

41 **A Strong Start**

44 Jefferson was born on April 13, 1743. At the age of nine, he began
58 to study Latin, Greek, and French. He would one day be able to speak
72 five languages and read seven.
77 When he went to school he studied law. In 1769 he was part of
91 the House of Burgesses, which was the first group of chosen law-
103 makers in our nation. While there, he was not known as a great public
116 speaker. It is not only spoken words that can make a change, though.
129 Sometimes written words can be just as valuable. People liked the
140 way he wrote about information from meetings while he was there.
151 They knew that he could write very well.
159 When the people wanted to be free from Britain, they asked
170 Jefferson to help. They asked him to write about why people wanted
182 to rebel against Britain. So he wrote the Declaration of Independence.

Name ______________________________

The Power of Words

The Declaration said that we are all created equal. It said that we all have certain rights, including "life, liberty, and the pursuit of happiness." This means that we should all have the right to freedom and happiness. Jefferson wrote these words when the people had a lot of criticism for British law. They wanted to be free from these laws. The people did not agree with the king. They wanted to protect their happiness. They wanted to be in charge of making their own laws.

The words that Jefferson wrote were the thoughts of many people. The people did not want to live under British rule. They felt that it was not fair. Instead, they wanted to have a life of liberty. They wanted a life where all people were equal, where people could search for happiness. This is why Jefferson wrote that if a government is not working, "it is the right of the people to alter or to abolish it." This meant that the people had the power. They could change how they were ruled.

Jefferson's words gave a voice to the people. His words filled them with optimism. His words gave them strength, too. The people felt ready to say they were free of Britain. The day on which they made this official is a special day. Do you know what day it is? It is the Fourth of July.

Jefferson was in law and politics. Yet, he is also known as a great writer. The Declaration that he wrote helped in the development of our nation. It came when the people needed it most. Without his strong words, America might not have been able to find its freedom when it did.

Name ____________________

A. Reread the passage and answer the questions.

1. Which detail in the first paragraph tells you what the author thinks Jefferson's biggest accomplishment is?

____

____

____

2. What does the seventh paragraph tell you about how the author feels about the words Jefferson wrote?

The authors feels they were filled with optimism and postive words.

3. How do your feelings about what Jefferson did for our country compare with the author's?

My feeling ares the same as the author.

B. Work with a partner. Read the passage aloud. Pay attention to expression. Stop after one minute. Fill out the chart.

	Words Read	–	Number of Errors	=	Words Correct Score
First Read		–		=	
Second Read		–		=	

Name ______________________________

Encouraging Change

President John F. Kennedy gives a speech to Congress in 1961.

John F. Kennedy did not plan to be a politician. He wanted to have a job in academics or the news. However, from 1947–1953 he was in the House of Representatives. He was a Senator from 1953–1960. In 1960 he was elected president. The words in his speech in 1961 helped bring change. He said, "Ask not what your country can do for you–ask what you can do for your country." He wanted people to better each other's lives.

Answer the questions about the text.

1. How do you know this text is a biography?

____

____

2. What text features does the text include?

____

3. What does the caption tell you about the photograph?

____

____

4. How do you know the photograph is a primary source?

____

____

Name ______________________________

Suffix	Meaning
-able	capable of
-ation	action or process
-ism	the act or state of
-ment	act or process of

Using the information in the box above, circle the word in each sentence below with a Latin or Greek suffix. Write the meaning of the word on the line. Use a dictionary if necessary.

1. He was the third president of the United States, but he might be best known for writing the Declaration of Independence.

____

2. Sometimes written words can be just as valuable.

____

3. People liked the way he wrote about information from meetings while he was there.

____

4. Jefferson wrote these words when the people had a lot of criticism for British law.

____

5. His words filled them with optimism.

____

6. What Jefferson wrote helped in the development of our nation.

____

Name ______________________________

A. Read each sentence. On the line, write the correct plural form of the noun in parentheses.

1. **(prop)** The play included many ______________ to make it look real.

2. **(hobby)** I have two ______________ that I enjoy doing after school.

3. **(mistake)** Did you make any ______________ on your homework?

4. **(moss)** There are different kinds of ______________ and plants.

5. **(arch)** We drove under two huge ______________ when we entered the city.

6. **(day)** There are seven ______________ in each week.

B. The suffixes *-ment, -ness, -age, -ance,* and *-ence* all mean "the state of" or "the act of" something. Write the meaning of each word below.

1. storage ______________

2. brightness ______________

3. punishment ______________

4. guidance ______________

5. patience ______________

6. excitement ______________

Name ____

A. Read the draft model. Use the questions that follow the draft to help you think about what details you can add to give the narrative a strong conclusion.

Draft Model

I had blamed my brother for ruining one of my books. He insisted that he hadn't even gone in my room. Then I saw the book's cover in our puppy's mouth. I learned an important lesson.

1. What details would tell why the narrator blamed the brother for ruining the book?
2. What did the puppy look like when the writer found it?
3. What details would provide a sense of closure and summarize the lesson the narrator learned?

B. Now revise the draft by adding a strong conclusion to help give readers a sense of closure.

____

____

____

____

____

____

____

____

Name ______________________________

Drew wrote the paragraphs below using text evidence from two different sources to answer the question: *How did Lincoln's words lead to change?*

Abraham Lincoln said what he believed. His words helped to end slavery. His speech at Gettysburg is famous.

When Lincoln ran for Senate, he spoke out against slavery. The author of *Abe's Honest Words* writes, "In speech after speech, he reminded people that slavery did not fit with the ideals of the Declaration of Independence."

Lincoln lost that race. Next, he ran for president. This time he was the winner. The Civil War soon broke out in 1861 and divided the country. Three years later, Lincoln used the Emancipation Proclamation to free African Americans in the South. Then he talked Congress into freeing all African Americans.

A major battle occurred in July of 1863 at Gettysburg, Pennsylvania. Several months later, Lincoln spoke there. The author of "A New Birth of Freedom," feels that Lincoln's Gettysburg Address is "one of the most famous speeches in our nation's history." Rappaport agrees. She writes that Lincoln's "words were there to guide those who chose to remember."

Abraham Lincoln said what he believed—and backed up his words with actions.

Reread the passage. Follow the directions below.

1. **Circle** a quotation from *Abe's Honest Words.*

2. **Draw a box** around text evidence from "A New Birth of Freedom."

3. **Underline** a detail that helps you understand the sequence of events in the Civil War.

4. **Write** an example of a linking verb that Drew uses on the line.

____

Name ______________________________

characteristics	concerns	disagreed	advancements
resistance	prevalent	inherit	agriculture

Finish each sentence using the vocabulary word provided.

1. **(characteristics)** Fruits such as lemons and limes ______________________________

______________________________.

2. **(prevalent)** During the wintertime ______________________________

______________________________.

3. **(agriculture)** She went to college to ______________________________

______________________________.

4. **(inherit)** Many parents hope their children ______________________________

______________________________.

5. **(disagreed)** Some of the fans at the soccer game ______________________________

______________________________.

6. **(concerns)** At the neighborhood meeting, ______________________________

______________________________.

7. **(advancements)** Computers and cell phones ______________________________

______________________________.

8. **(resistance)** To avoid getting sick, ______________________________

______________________________.

Name ____________________

Read the selection. Complete the author's point of view graphic organizer.

Details

↓

Author's Point of View

Name ____

Read the passage. Use the reread strategy to help you understand the text.

Is Nuclear Energy Safe?

Atoms are the tiny things that make up everything in the universe.
12 At the center of an atom is the nucleus. The energy that holds the
26 nucleus together is called nuclear energy. Scientists have discovered
35 how to use that energy as power in our everyday lives. This energy is
49 cheap and clean. But there are dangers as well.

58 **Going Nuclear**

60 In the 1930s, physicists learned how to use the energy inside atoms.
72 They split the atom. This released a huge amount of energy. This was
85 exciting to many people. We get much of our power from oil and coal.
99 But people knew that oil and coal would not last forever. Nuclear
111 energy was much easier to come by. It was a great discovery!
123 Nuclear power plants have many benefits. They do not release
133 harmful chemicals into the air. The waste that is produced is in solid
146 form. This makes it easier to control. Also, there is a very small
159 amount of waste compared to other ways of making energy.
169 Nuclear power plants last much longer than coal plants. They can
180 sometimes last sixty years. Plus, nuclear power plants use only a tiny
192 amount of fuel to make energy. That means we could make nuclear
204 energy for many generations.

Name ______________________________

Problems with Waste

Sadly, there are serious problems with nuclear power. The first problem is the waste that is produced. It is true, the waste is very small. Yet it is highly toxic. Physicians have discovered it can cause severe illness. It has to be contained. Sometimes though, the waste leaks out. It can get into drinking water. The waste can cause cancer in humans.

Japan Earthquake Disaster

It is true that accidents are rare. However, they can be very bad if they happen. In 2011, there was a large earthquake in Japan. As a result, one of the nuclear power plants was destroyed. The event is too recent to know all the effects it might have. Still, scientists believe that when the disaster is finally chronicled, it will prove to be one of the worst nuclear disasters ever.

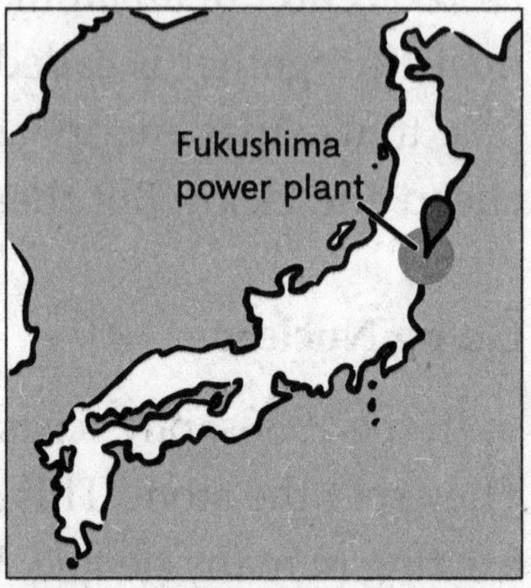

Five days after the earthquake, the U.S. government advised Americans within 50 miles of the plant to leave.

Thousands of people had to be moved away from the plant. Waste leaked into the ocean. The cleanup will be long. It will take decades and it will be very costly.

Being Careful

There is no doubt that nuclear energy can be very good. It can give us energy. It can be safe and cheap. But it can also be dangerous. If we must use it, then we must use it carefully.

Name ______________________________

A. Reread the passage and answer the questions.

1. According to paragraph 2, what is one way that nuclear energy is better than energy from coal and oil?

____

____

2. According to paragraphs 3 and 4, what is one of the benefits of nuclear power?

____

____

3. List two problems with nuclear energy that the author names in the text.

____

____

____

4. What is the author's point of view on nuclear energy?

____

____

B. Work with a partner. Read the passage aloud. Pay attention to rate. Stop after one minute. Fill out the chart.

	Words Read	–	Number of Errors	=	Words Correct Score
First Read		–		=	
Second Read		–		=	

Name ____________________

Should We Use a Virus to Stop Fire Ants?

The fire ant has been an unwelcome guest in the United States ever since its arrival in 1930. Each year, fire ant colonies cause billions of dollars of damage. This much money could be put to better use.

Luckily, scientists have discovered a virus that may help control fire ant colonies. The SINV-1 virus is capable of destroying an infected colony in three months. Scientists' efforts to turn SINV-1 into a pesticide will save citizens a lot of money.

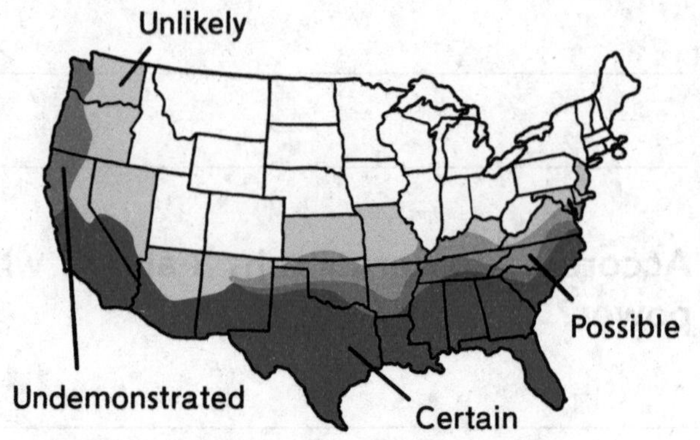

Possible Range of the Fire Ant

Answer the questions about the text.

1. How do you know this text is a persuasive article?

It tells scientists have made a virus.

2. What is the author's opinion about the SINV-1 virus?

I think the auther is terjines to get us to think that is trow.

3. What text feature is included? According to the text feature, how is the range of the fire ant changing?

A map is the text futare. I think the dark is were they are most at

Name ______________________________

<u>Greek Root Meanings</u>

phys - nature or body

dec - ten

gen - birth or kind

chron - time

Read each passage below. Use the Greek roots from the box above along with context clues to find the meaning of each word in bold. Write the meaning on the line.

1. In the 1930s, **physicists** learned how to use the energy inside atoms. They split the atom.

____

2. Nuclear power plants last much longer than coal plants. They can sometimes last sixty years. Plus, nuclear power plants use only a tiny amount of fuel to make energy. That means we could make nuclear energy for many **generations**.

____

3. Waste leaked into the ocean. The cleanup will be long. It will take **decades** and it will be very costly.

____

4. A nuclear weapon was used in World War II. John Hersey **chronicled** the events in his true story, *Hiroshima*.

____

Name ____

A. Read each sentence and circle the compound word. Then write the meaning of the compound word based on the smaller words.

1. There was a terrible snowstorm yesterday.

   Meaning: ____

2. This new jacket is both warm and waterproof.

   Meaning: ____

3. Did you like to eat peanut butter and jelly sandwiches?

   Meaning: ____

4. She jumped off the diving board and landed with a splash.

   Meaning: ____

B. Read the words in the box. Sort them under their related roots below.

refresher	movement	collection	familiarize
collectible	unfamiliar	freshen	remove

collect

1. ____________________

2. ____________________

family

3. ____________________

4. ____________________

fresh

5. ____________________

6. ____________________

move

7. ____________________

8. ____________________

Name ______________________________

A. Read the draft model. Use the questions that follow the draft to help you think about the writer's audience.

Draft Model

Technology is cool. It's got this way of making things easier. It does stuff like help people keep up with pals and find important info.

1. Who might be the audience for this writing?

2. What words and details could be added or deleted to make the purpose clearer?

3. What words in the model could be replaced to create a more formal tone?

4. What words and details could be added or deleted to appeal to the audience even more?

B. Now revise the draft by adding or replacing language to make the tone more formal.

____

____

____

____

____

____

____

Name ______________________________

Cristina wrote the paragraphs below using text evidence from two different sources to answer the question: *In your opinion, is it better to rely on GM seeds to grow crops, or is it better to rely on the methods that Chris Stevens did in growing his pumpkin?*

When growing crops, I think it is better to rely on the methods that Chris Stephens used to grow his pumpkins in "The Pick of the Patch." Chris Stephens won the world record for the biggest pumpkin without using GM seeds. He used good quality soil, fertilized his pumpkins, and protected them from bugs and wind.

The farmer in *A New Kind of Corn* says that he prefers to grow Bt corn, a genetically modified food. He says that he no longer has to spray his fields with pesticides. I understand his point, but nobody knows what the long-term consequences are of eating GM foods. In fact, some tests have shown that mice developed stomach lesions from eating GM foods. So when I decide to grow crops, I will rely on the methods of Chris Stephens.

Reread the passage. Follow the directions below.

1. **Underline** an example of text evidence that Cristina used to support her opinion.

2. **Draw a box** around the text evidence that shows Cristina using a formal voice to appeal to her audience and purpose.

3. **Circle** the transition Cristina used to connect her opinion with reasons.

4. **Write** an irregular verb that Christina uses.

____

Name ________________________________

democracy	commitment	privilege	legislation
version	eventually	amendments	compromise

Use a word from the box to answer each question. Then use the word in a sentence.

1. What word might describe an agreement reached by two different sides?

____

____

2. What is a system of government where the people decide what happens?

____

3. If there are formal changes made to a law, what are the changes called?

____

____

4. What is another word for *finally*? ________________

____

5. If a community creates its own laws, what is it responsible for? ________

____

6. What is another word for *a sense of obligation*? ________________

____

7. What do you call a special right that a person has? ________________

____

8. What is another word for *an account given in a particular way*?

____

Name ______________________________

Read the selection. Complete the cause and effect graphic organizer.

Cause	→	Effect
	→	
	→	
	→	
	→	

Name ____

Read the passage. Use the ask and answer questions strategy to understand difficult parts of the text.

We the People

Ms. Quibble stood by the chalkboard in front of her fourth-grade
11 class. "Who can tell me why the American colonies wanted to
22 separate from England and become their own country?"
30 The class was quiet. Some students scribbled in their notebooks
40 or shuffled their feet. Finally, a single hand shot up. Ms. Quibble
52 adjusted her spectacles. "Yes, Kwan?"
57 "People wanted to separate because they wanted liberty,"
65 Kwan said. "They felt that they didn't have a voice in the British
78 government."
79 "Very good!" Ms. Quibble said. "What was the name of the
90 document that declared the colonies' freedom?"
96 Kwan was the only volunteer. "It was the Declaration of
106 Independence," she said.
109 "Kwan, I can tell you will ace this test." Ms. Quibble sounded
121 impressed. "I *highly* suggest that everyone else study during lunch."
131 Sam Jones ran to catch up with Kwan after class. "You sure know a
145 lot about history," he said.
150 "That's because I'm studying for my naturalization exam. I've been
160 memorizing a lot about America," she said.
167 "Your *what* exam?" Sam asked.
172 "It's a test to become an American citizen," Kwan said. "My
183 parents have been studying with me for months. We are so excited for
196 the chance to become citizens!"

Name ______________________________

The Document that Launched a Country

Sam and Kwan sat together at lunch. They inspected a copy of the Constitution that was printed in their textbooks. Kwan explained that the Constitution sets the rules for the government. It also explains the three branches of government. The legislative branch makes laws. The executive branch makes sure laws are followed. The judicial branch makes sense of the laws.

"All of the branches have checks and balances on each other," Kwan said. "This is so no one branch has complete power."

Tetra Images/Corbis

To amend the Constitution, both houses of Congress or three-fourths of the states must approve.

Rights for All People

"I'm still not sure why a piece of paper from hundreds of years ago is still so important," Sam said.

"Do you know the first three words of the Constitution, Sam?"

"We the people..."

"Right! The government of the United States is supposed to speak for all the people in every community. But there are times when the government has needed to make a change or addition to the Constitution. We call these changes *amendments*. The Bill of Rights is made up of the first ten amendments to the Constitution. Do you know what the Bill of Rights is?"

"I think it gives Americans freedoms, like the freedoms of speech and religion," Sam said.

"Exactly! So, the Bill of Rights makes sure everyone is free."

Sam and Kwan placed their trays on the cafeteria counter. "Good luck on the test today, Sam. I think you're going to do great," Kwan said and winked.

Name ____

A. Reread the passage and answer the questions.

1. What is the cause in the following sentence from the passage?
People wanted to separate because they wanted liberty.

____

____

2. What is the effect in the following sentence from the passage?
People wanted to separate because they wanted liberty.

____

____

3. In paragraphs 8–10, what is the cause of the situation Kwan describes? What is the effect?

____

____

____

B. Work with a partner. Read the passage aloud. Pay attention to phrasing and rate. Stop after one minute. Fill out the chart.

	Words Read	–	Number of Errors	=	Words Correct Score
First Read		–		=	
Second Read		–		=	

Name Maron

An Interview with a State Representative

"I know that your main responsibilities are writing bills and voting them into effect. Do you have any other responsibilities?" I asked the representative.

"Like every other representative, I serve on two **committees** (kuh•MIT•tees)," he told me.

"What does a committee do?" I asked.

"A committee is a group of Congress members. They study a specific subject, like the military or education, and become experts on that subject. When a bill related to that subject is written, the committee reads the bill. Then it reports to Congress on the bill. Each committee provides valuable advice about changes that should be made to bills before they are passed."

Answer the questions about the text.

1. **How do you know this text is narrative nonfiction?**

I know this is narrative nonfiction because it didn't hapen but it could hapen.

2. **What text features are included in this piece of narrative nonfiction?**

The text features are a titele and a bold word

3. **Choose one text feature. How does it add to your understanding of this text?**

The titele helps me know what the story is going to be about

4. **What opinion does the author express in the text?**

The auther expresses that he know committes write bills and vote.

Name ______________________________

Latin Root	Meaning
commun	common
mem	remember
nat	to be from
scrib	write
spect	look

A. Look at each word below and identify the Latin root. Circle the roots and write the meaning of each word. Use the information above to help you.

1. community ______________________________
2. scribbled ______________________________
3. spectacles ______________________________
4. naturalization ______________________________
5. memorizing ______________________________
6. inspected ______________________________

B. Using what you know about the roots *spect* and *scrib,* write the meaning of each word below. Use a dictionary, if necessary.

7. spectator

____

8. inscribe

____

Name ______________________________

A. Read each verb. Then write the correct *-ed* and *-ing* forms for each verb.

Verb	+ *ed*	+ *ing*
1. scare	________	________
2. tap	________	________
3. discuss	________	________
4. taste	________	________
5. force	________	________
6. skip	________	________

B. Read each word. Draw a slanted line (/) to divide it into syllables. Then write the vowel team on the line.

1. coaster ________
2. bookend ________
3. repeat ________
4. southwest ________
5. needle ________
6. unload ________

Name ______________________________

A. Read the draft model. Use the questions that follow the draft to help you think about the topic sentence and the supporting sentences.

Draft Model

Schools have rules. Games have rules. There are rules in my home also. I have to clean my room once a week.

1. What is the topic of the draft model? What would be a clearer way to state it?

2. What words could you add to show how the supporting sentences relate to the main idea?

3. What other supporting sentences could you add to strengthen the text?

B. Now revise the draft by adding a topic sentence and supporting sentences to help readers learn more about the importance of rules.

____

____

____

____

____

____

____

____

Name ____________________

Malia wrote the paragraph below using text evidence from two different sources to answer the question: *In your opinion, can kids participate in our democracy?*

I think that kids can participate in our democracy even though they cannot vote. Only people over 18 years of age have the right to vote, according to "The Birth of American Democracy." However, kids can play a part in other ways, like influencing the legislative branch to pass laws. If children put enough pressure on members of government to do something, then change can really happen! For example, in *See How They Run,* a group of second graders proposed to the state legislature that the ladybug should be the official state insect. After the students worked hard promoting it, the governor signed it into law and the ladybug became the state insect. In addition, a group of children in New York started a group called Kids Against Pollution to raise money to help pay for the cleanup of toxic dump sites. After seven years, the state finally passed a law to clean up the toxic waste sites. This is why I believe kids are able to participate in our democracy.

Reread the passage. Follow the directions below.

1. **Underline** the text evidence that tells why kids cannot vote.

2. **Circle** an example of a transition word that links a supporting detail to Malia's opinion.

3. **Draw a box around** a detail that shows Kids Against Pollution was successful.

4. **I think that kids can participate in our democracy even though they cannot vote.**
   Write the pronoun and antecedent that matches it in this sentence on the line.

   ____

Name ______________________________

accompanies	campaign	governor	intend
opponent	overwhelming	tolerate	weary

Use the context clues in each sentence to help you decide which vocabulary word fits best in the blank.

Elections don't happen every year, so getting to vote is very important for my dad. When the ________________ begins to show who may be the next ________________ of our state, my dad becomes very involved. He usually has a favorite, but he always learns about the ________________ so he has all information to make a good decision.

The amount of election mail we get is ________________, but my dad carefully goes through it all. He won't ________________ it if we tell him we are ________________ of all the news he watches. He insists on knowing as much as possible.

Every Election Day, we ________________ to go together so he can vote after he gets off of work. But every time, he comes home and has already voted. He likes the little "I Voted" sticker that ________________ him through his day. He says he has done his duty as a United States citizen, and that makes him happy.

Name ____

Read the selection. Complete the point of view graphic organizer.

Details

↓

Point of View

Name ______________________________

Read the passage. Use the make predictions strategy to predict what will happen later on in the text.

The Sheep in the Wilderness

Our herd of sheep was ruled by a cruel shepherd for years. At last
14 we couldn't stand it any longer. We began to stay awake each night
27 until the shepherd had gone to bed. Then we would plan our escape.
40 Finally, the time came to make our move. Late one night, our herd
53 crept quietly out of the pasture while the shepherd and his dogs slept.
66 *We are finally free*! I thought as we entered the dark forest.
78 Life was hard when we lived with the shepherd, but I learned that it
92 was even harder on our own. Trouble came when we needed to find a
106 place to graze. Our group came to a fork in the path. "There's a wide,
121 green pasture that way," an old gray sheep said, pointing to the path
134 that led downhill. "I remember the shepherd took us there once to
146 graze. There was plenty for everyone to eat."
154 "We can't go there!" a younger brown sheep said. "If the shepherd
166 took you to graze in that pasture, he knows where it is. Besides, it's
180 completely surrounded by forest. We would never see the shepherd
190 coming if he tried to sneak up on us." The brown sheep pointed to
204 the other path. It led uphill. "There are fewer trees on the mountain.
217 There must be a pasture there. And if the shepherd comes looking for
230 us, we'll see him before he sees us."

Name ____

Each of the other sheep took the side of either the old gray sheep or the young brown sheep. The herd argued for hours, but we still could not decide where to graze. Finally we all got so tired of arguing that we fell asleep.

Just before I fell asleep, I had an idea. We could choose one sheep to be our leader! This sheep could hear the other sheep's ideas and decide what to do. This way, we wouldn't have to spend all of our time arguing. I would tell the other sheep in the morning.

When I woke up, the others had already taken up where they had left off and were arguing over where to graze. So I shouted, "Quiet, everyone!" The herd fell silent and looked at me.

"We can't argue every time we need to make a decision," I began. "We need to choose someone we trust to lead us. This sheep will listen to our ideas and make the most important decisions for us. We may not like every decision our leader makes, but at least our voices will be heard. And if we choose a new leader each month, the sheep who feel that their voices aren't being heard will have another chance to share their ideas."

The herd liked my idea, so we set out to choose a leader. The sheep would vote by putting a brown leaf into a pile if they wanted the young ram to lead, a green leaf if they wanted the old gray sheep, and a red leaf if they wanted me. Each sheep voted. When we counted the leaves, I had won the most votes!

Name ____

A. Reread the passage and answer the questions.

1. What kind of narrator tells the story? How do you know?

____

____

____

2. Is the narrator part of the story? What do we learn about the narrator in the first paragraph?

____

____

____

3. What is the narrator's point of view about leadership? Cite evidence from the text.

____

____

____

B. Work with a partner. Read the passage aloud. Pay attention to phrasing and expression. Stop after one minute. Fill out the chart.

	Words Read	–	Number of Errors	=	Words Correct Score
First Read		–		=	
Second Read		–		=	

Name ____

The *Aurora's* First Mission

Construction on the *Aurora* ended in 2412. Over a mile in length, it was unlike any space cruiser ever built. The ship's advanced computer controlled the billions of instruments on board. Now the ship needed a captain. Two candidates were favored. Dr. Yanic had designed the ship's computer. He knew how it worked and how to fix it. The other candidate, Admiral Clark, had been in the Galactic Navy and knew how to run a ship.

Answer the questions about the text.

1. How do you know this text is fantasy?

____

2. What in the text could not happen in real life?

____

____

3. What text feature is included?

____

4. How does the text feature help show that the text is fantasy?

____

____

Name ______________________________

Read each passage. Underline the words that help you figure out the meaning of each idiom in bold. Then write the idiom's meaning on the line.

1. Finally, the time came to **make our move**. Late one night, our herd crept quietly out of the pasture while the shepherd and his dogs slept.

____

____

2. Life was hard when we lived with the shepherd, but I learned that it was even harder **on our own**.

____

____

3. Each of the other sheep **took the side of** either the old gray sheep or the young brown sheep. The herd argued for hours, but we still could not decide where to graze.

____

____

Name ______________________________

A. Change the *y* to *i* and add the indicated ending to each word. Write the new word on the line.

1. empty + er = emptier
2. sorry + est = sorriest
3. reply + ed = replied
4. carry + es = carries
5. funny + er = funnier
6. silly + est = silliest

B. Read each sentence. Underline the word with an *r*-controlled vowel syllable. Then circle the *r*-controlled vowel syllable.

1. I think this is the best birthday present she has given me.
2. The small boat dropped its anchor late last night.
3. I put a leash and collar on my dog when we take a walk.
4. We went to see the mayor make an election speech.
5. My brother finished his juice and then went to bed.

Name ______________________________

A. Read the draft model. Use the questions that follow the draft to help you think about using dialogue to develop characters.

Draft Model

Today, I gave a speech at the rally. I talked about some of the changes I plan to make as mayor. I talked about improving our parks.

1. **Where could dialogue be added to help bring the narrator to life?**

2. **What dialogue could be added to reveal exactly what the narrator is thinking?**

3. **What other details of the narrator's plans could be revealed through dialogue?**

B. Now revise the draft by using dialogue to develop the main character in the story.

____

____

____

____

____

____

____

____

Name ____

Ricky used text evidence from two different sources to respond to the prompt: *Write an email from Ike LaRue to Florida State Senator Anthony C. Hill. Explain why Ike wants Senator Hill to reduce class sizes at dog obedience schools.*

Dear Senator Hill,

Thank you for passing a bill to reduce class sizes for Florida students. However, many Florida dogs are in large classes, too. We need you to help us! Dogs may not be able to vote, but their humans do. (My human, Mrs. LaRue loves to vote–almost as much as she loves me!)

We need your help in passing the following law: *No obedience school shall put more than four dogs in one class.* No one can learn how to protect their humans from dangerous criminals or rescue frozen travelers if they're crammed in a class with too many other barking, panting canines.

Not all dogs are suited for such noble work. Some just need a little training so they don't run off with the ball during a baseball game or juicy sausages from a butcher shop. All dogs can use some training–but they'll learn more when they're taught in small classes!

Signed,
Ike LaRue

Reread the passage. Follow the directions below.

1. **Circle** the part that explains why Ike is writing to Senator Hill.
2. **Draw a box** around a detail that describes Ike's own behavior.
3. **Underline** a detail that tells what Senator Hill did for Florida students.
4. **We need you to help us!**
   Write the subject and object pronouns in the sentence on the line.

   ____

Name ______________________

gleaming	decade	tinkering	engineering
scouted	squirmed	directing	technology

Use a word from the box to answer each question. Then use the word in a sentence.

1. What did the boy do when he twisted his body to avoid being tagged?
The boy squirmed so he was not tagged.

2. What word describes what a light is doing when it is shining?
The light is gleaming in the darck.

3. What profession uses scientific knowledge for practical use? Engineering is profession uses scientific knowledge for practical use.

4. What did the eagle do when it flew in search of food? The eagle scouted for food.

5. What is another word for a *period of ten years*? Ten years is a decade

6. What is the coach doing when he is giving instructions to the team?
The coach was directing his team.

7. What is another word for puttering? Another word for puttering is tinkering.

8. What word means *the use of science for practical purposes*? Technology means the use of science for practical

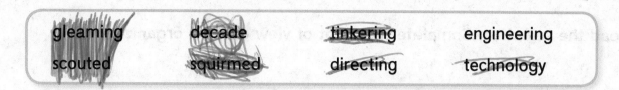

Name ____

Read the selection. Complete the point of view graphic organizer.

Details

Point of View

Name ____

Read the passage. Use the make predictions strategy to help you make predictions about what will happen next.

Leonardo's Mechanical Knight

Leonardo scrambled out of bed early one clear spring day in 1464.
12 He was excited to get out to the barn where he was working on a new
28 invention.
29 For months he had begged and pleaded with his father to get him a
43 suit of armor. On April 15—Leonardo's twelfth birthday—he got his
55 wish! He had set the armor up in the barn that day. The barn quickly
70 filled with Leonardo's notes and equipment as he worked and toiled
81 on his new invention: a mechanical knight.
88 High atop a rickety ladder, Leonardo was deep in concentration.
98 All his focus was on fixing the mechanical knight's arm, but it wasn't
111 easy work. No matter what he did, the knight's arm refused to lift!
124 Leonardo frowned and scowled at it.
130 "Leonardo!" yelled a voice. He jumped in surprise and shock as the
142 ladder teetered and shook under his feet.
149 "Oh no!" he exclaimed, losing his balance. He tumbled off the
160 ladder and into a pile of hay. The mechanical knight's arm lay broken
173 on the ground.
176 His good friend Albiera peered down at him. "Leonardo, are you
187 all right?"
189 "I'm fine," he said. He wasn't hurt, just upset that his mechanical
201 knight was broken.
204 Albiera glanced at the knight with the missing arm, the stacks of
216 notebooks, and the piles of papers. "What on earth are you doing in
229 here?" she asked.
232 "I was working on a new invention, but it's not going so well."

Name ______________________________

Albiera knew the best way to cheer Leonardo up was to get him talking about his favorite subject: science. She picked up the mechanical knight's arm from the ground. "This looks interesting. Will you tell me about it?"

Sure enough, Leonardo's face lit up in a smile.

"This is my new invention. It's a mechanical knight," he said. "Watch what it can do!"

He cranked a handle behind the mechanical knight and stepped back to watch. Suddenly, the mechanical knight began to move on its own! It turned its head from side to side. It opened and closed its mouth. The attached arm clicked and ticked as it rose above the mechanical knight's head.

Albiera clapped her hands. "*Bravo!* That's amazing!"

"It's a simple system of pulleys and levers," he said in a humble voice.

"Don't be so modest. I've never seen anything like it before!"

"It's not finished yet. When it's completed, my mechanical knight will sit up, and maybe even walk, just as a human does."

"That would be quite a feat! But I don't understand what you can do with a mechanical knight. Why do we need machines like this at all?" asked Albiera.

Leonardo's face brightened with excitement. "There are so many reasons! Just think about it. A mechanical person will go where we can't go. A machine could explore the bottom of the sea or even the stars! There's so much we could learn from machines."

Albiera laughed. "You have such crazy ideas, Leonardo!"

"You never know," he said. "One day there might be a machine that helps people fly!"

Name ______________________________

A. Reread the passage and answer the questions.

1. What pronouns are used in the first two paragraphs? Which character do these pronouns refer to?

We see he, him, and his father refer to Leonardo.

2. What kind of narrator tells the story? Is the narrator part of the story?

It is thrid person No the narrator is not in the story

3. In paragraph 7, how is Leonardo feeling? In paragraph 10, what does Albiera do to make Leonardo feel better?

He is feeling down
she asks about science

4. What is the narrator's point of view about machines? Cite evidence from the text.

The narrator point of view is that machines are cool. The story said he was exicted.

B. Work with a partner. Read the passage aloud. Pay attention to expression. Stop after one minute. Fill out the chart.

	Words Read	–	Number of Errors	=	Words Correct Score
First Read		–		=	
Second Read		–		=	

Name ______________________________

Starting Work on the Brooklyn Bridge

I met the head of my work crew, Mr. Calloway. He told me about the caissons on the bridge's foundations, where I'll be working.

"The caissons are locked chambers at the bottom of the river, where workers dig down to the bedrock so the foundations can be placed. The pay's good because it's so dangerous down there," Mr. Calloway said.

"Dangerous? Because of flooding?" I asked.

"No, because the caissons are filled with high-pressure air to keep water from filling the work area," Mr. Calloway replied. "Some guys work down in the caissons too long and come to the surface too fast. The change in pressure gives them terrible pains, called caisson disease. It has killed two workers since 1870," Mr. Calloway explained.

Answer the questions about the text.

1. How do you know this text is historical fiction?

We Know this text is historicall fiction because thuir is dates and made up chartorzs.

2. During which historical event does the story take place?

The story takes place at the Brooklyn Bridge

3. What literary element is included in this piece of historical fiction?

____

4. What does the literary element add to your understanding of the text?

____

____

Name ______________________________

Read each passage. Underline the synonym that helps you figure out the meaning of each word in bold. Then write the definition of the word in bold on the line.

1. For months he had begged and **pleaded** with his father to get him a suit of armor.

____

2. The barn quickly filled with Leonardo's notes and equipment as he worked and **toiled** on his new invention: a mechanical knight.

____

3. High atop a rickety ladder, Leonardo was deep in **concentration**. All his focus was on fixing the mechanical knight's arm, but it wasn't easy work.

____

4. No matter what he did, the knight's arm refused to lift! Leonardo frowned and **scowled** at it.

____

5. "It's a simple system of pulleys and levers," he said in a **humble** voice. "Don't be so modest. I've never seen anything like it before!"

____

Name ______________________________

A. Read the words in the box below. Sort the words based on their vowel sounds.

bruised	huge	should	issue	crook	stoop

Vowel sound in *spoon*	Vowel sound in *cube*	Vowel sound in *book*
1. ____________	3. ____________	5. ____________
2. ____________	4. ____________	6. ____________

B. Divide each word into its syllables with a slanted line (/). Then write the consonant + *le* syllable on the line. Remember that an *le* syllable may also be spelled with a consonant + *al, el, il,* or *ol.*

1. tonsil ____________

2. formal ____________

3. tumble ____________

4. bridle ____________

5. symbol ____________

6. channel ____________

Name ______________________________

A. Read the draft model. Use the questions that follow the draft to help you think about adding setting details to develop the plot.

Draft Model

I woke up and went downstairs for breakfast. My brother and I went swimming in the lake. Then we went to help our dad with the horses in the barn. After that, we all went inside to do household chores.

1. What details could be added to show when and where the story takes place?
2. What setting details could describe the lake?
3. How could you better describe the barn?
4. How could setting details be strengthened to help drive the plot of the story?

B. Now revise the draft by adding details about the setting to help develop the story's plot.

____

____

____

____

____

____

____

____

Name ______________________________

Patrice wrote the dialogue below using text evidence from two different sources to respond to the prompt: *Write a dialogue between Mae and Gramps in which she tells him how the space program can help them on the farm.*

"Gramps, some of the things the astronauts use in space can help us here on the farm," I said to him.

"Really? How do you figure that?" Gramps asked.

"Well," I began, "I was reading that the material used in the astronauts' space suits can be used as air cushion soles in shoes. Just think, Gramps, with those air cushion soles in your boots, your feet won't be so sore at the end of the day!"

"Is that so?" he asked with a small amount of interest in his voice.

"Yes, and that's not all. You know how we always have to put the watermelon on ice to keep it cold? Well, the astronauts have ways of keeping their foods safe from spoiling in all kinds of temperatures. And someday we'll use that new technology to keep our food from spoiling!"

Now I see a smile forming on Gramp's lips. "I reckon that's something," he said.

Reread the passage. Follow the directions below.

1. **Underline** the sentence that establishes the topic of the narrative.

2. **Draw a box** around the dialogue that shows that Mae has convinced Gramps that things from the space program can help him.

3. **Circle** one of the details from *The Moon Over Star* in the dialogue.

4. **Now I see a smile forming on Gramp's lips.**
   Rewrite the sentence above using the pronoun *she*.

   ____

Name ______________________________

rotates	crescent	sliver	astronomer
telescope	series	phases	specific

Finish each sentence using the vocabulary word provided.

1. **(phases)** The large apartment building next door to us ______________________________ ______________________________.

2. **(astronomer)** Since she likes studying the planets and stars, ______________________________ ______________________________.

3. **(series)** There was a ______________________________ ______________________________.

4. **(rotates)** I like when the basketball player ______________________________ ______________________________.

5. **(specific)** We arrived at his house ______________________________ ______________________________.

6. **(telescope)** I discovered a new star ______________________________ ______________________________.

7. **(sliver)** We avoided stepping on glass at the beach ______________________________ ______________________________.

8. **(crescent)** We looked up at the night sky ______________________________ ______________________________.

Name ____

Read the selection. Complete the cause and effect graphic organizer.

Cause	→	**Effect**
	→	
	→	
	→	
	→	

Name ______________________________

Read the passage. Use the ask and answer questions strategy to understand new information in the text.

Stars: Lights in the Night Sky

Long ago, people thought the stars were lights attached to a big
12 dome over Earth. The stars moved across the sky each night.
23 As a result, it looked as if the dome were rotating around Earth.
36 But now we know that this isn't true. Stars are actually huge,
48 glowing balls of plasma, or ionized atoms. Some stars look like
59 little pinpricks. Most are so far away that they can't be seen with the
73 naked eye.

75 **What's a Star?**

78 Stars are made of a mixture of plasmas like hydrogen. As you can
91 imagine, a star's core is extremely hot. When lots of pressure squeezes
103 the star's hot center, the hydrogen changes into helium. This process
114 produces lots of energy. As a result, the star shines a bright light
127 through space.

129 When you look up at the stars, you may think that most of them
143 produce a white light. Take another look. Stars generally lie on a
155 color spectrum. This range of colors goes from red to yellow to blue.
168 But what do the colors mean? Well, blue stars are much hotter. If you
182 compare the two stars Betelgeuse (BEE-tehl-jooz) and Rigel
190 (RIGH-jehl), you will see that Betelgeuse is reddish and Rigel is
201 bluish. Rigel has the higher core temperature.

Name ______________________

The Sun

The sun is the star at the center of our solar system. It looks bigger than other stars. That's because it's closer to Earth. The sun is actually an ordinary, middle-aged star. If you compare the actual size of the sun to the sizes of other stars, you'll realize that the sun is quite average. But the sun does a huge job for a star its size. It provides Earth with most of the energy it needs to support life. Without the sun, Earth would be just a barren rock floating in space! None of the life now on Earth's surface could exist.

Turning Out the Lights

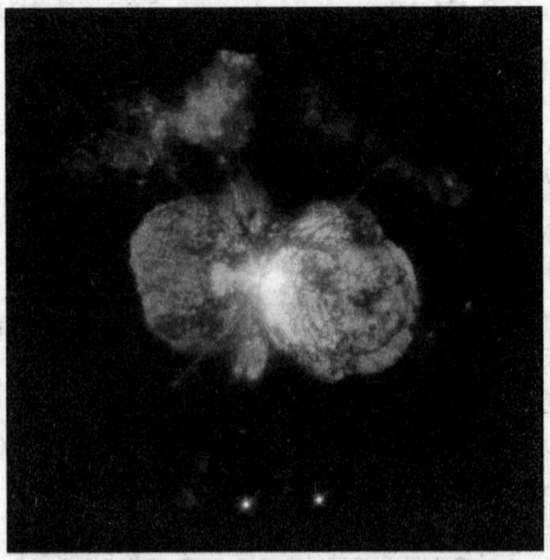

NASA, ESA, and the Hubble SM4 ERO Team

After a large star goes supernova, it may become a black hole.

Stars don't last forever. After billions of years, a star will use up all its hydrogen. A small star simply stops shining. This will happen to the sun one day. Of course, this won't happen for billions of years.

A large star, however, ends in a big explosion. When a star does this, it is called a supernova (soo-per-NO-va). After the explosion, all of the star's material gets crushed and stops shining. Especially large stars will then become large objects called black holes. In a black hole, the crushed material becomes so dense that it develops a gravitational (grav-i-TAY-shun-al) pull strong enough to keep even light from escaping. To this day, we still don't know what happens in a black hole.

The sun and other stars have fascinated astronomers for centuries. Stars light up the sky at night, and they make life on Earth possible. But they have a life of their own. Next time you're out on a clear night, look up at the stars. Which one do you think might be the next supernova?

Name ______________________________

Read each passage below. Underline the context clues that help you understand the meaning of each word in bold. Then write the definition for each word on the line.

1. Stars are made of a mixture of plasmas like hydrogen. As you can imagine, a star's **core** is extremely hot. When lots of pressure squeezes the star's hot center, the hydrogen changes into helium.

____

2. When you look up at the stars, you may think that most of them produce a white light. Take another look. Stars generally lie on a color **spectrum**. This range of colors goes from red to yellow to blue.

____

3. The sun does a huge job for a star its size. It provides Earth with most of the energy it needs to support life. Without the sun, Earth would be just a **barren** rock floating in space! None of the life now on Earth's surface could exist.

____

4. A large star ends in a big explosion. When a star does this, it is called a **supernova**. After the explosion, all of the star's material gets crushed and stops shining.

____

5. In a black hole, the crushed material becomes so dense that it develops a **gravitational** pull strong enough to keep even light from escaping.

____

Name ______________________

A. Read each sentence. Circle the word with the same vowel sound found in *boy* or *cow*. Then write the letters that make the vowel sound on the line.

1. The voices in the hall would make it hard to study for the test. __________
2. The tree will tower over the plants once it begins to grow. __________
3. I must carefully pack for the long voyage ahead of me. __________
4. There were over two thousand people at the show last night. __________
5. The students were howling with laughter at my comedy act. __________
6. The icy snow was beginning to annoy the birds in the tree. __________

B. Read the definitions below. Then read each word and circle the Greek or Latin root. Write the meaning of the root on the line.

The Greek root *graph* means "write." The Latin root *spec* means "look."
The Greek root *phon* means "sound." The Latin root *aqua* means "water."

1. megaphone ______________
2. speculate ______________
3. aquamarine ______________
4. geography ______________
5. inspection ______________
6. homograph ______________

Name ______________________________

A. Read the draft model. Use the questions that follow the draft to help you think about using figurative language to help the reader visualize the text.

Draft Model

The night sky is dark. The stars twinkle high in the sky. Sometimes there are clouds in the sky. The stars are reflected in rivers and lakes.

1. What figurative language could be added to describe the night sky?
2. What figurative language could be used to describe the clouds?
3. What other figurative language could be used to help readers visualize the scene?

B. Now revise the draft by adding figurative language to help readers visualize the night sky.

____

____

____

____

____

____

____

____

Name ____________________

Jason used text evidence from *Why Does the Moon Change Shape?* and "How It Came to Be" to respond to the prompt: *Compare how the two sources explain daylight.*

Why Does the Moon Change Shape? is an informative text. "How It Came to Be" includes two myths. Both sources explain daylight but in very different ways.

In *Why Does the Moon Change Shape?* the author presents facts. Earth orbits, or moves around the Sun. Our planet also rotates, or spins, as it orbits. Daylight occurs when part of Earth faces the Sun.

The Greek myth, "Why the Sun Travels Across the Sky," was written long ago. People didn't have tools to study the sky, so they created myths to explain natural events. In this myth, Helios, a god, causes day and night. The myth describes, "rays of brilliant light" pouring from Helios's crown as he climbed into the sky in a "shining" chariot with four horses. Helios and his chariot are as hot and bright as the Sun as they cross the sky.

One source presents facts, and the other tells a good story.

Reread the passage. Follow the directions below.

1. **Underline** a fact that explains why there is daylight.
2. **Draw a box** around one of the words Jason uses to describe the Earth's movement.
3. **Circle** an example of a simile that Jason uses.
4. **Write** one of the possessive pronouns Jason uses on the line.

____

Name ______________________________

attain	dangling	hovering	triumph

Use the context clues in each sentence to help you decide which vocabulary word fits best in the blank.

When we left for our walk that morning, I never thought that I would be making history. I happened to grab my camera that was ________________ off my doorknob by its strap before we left for the woods, and it was a lucky chance! About an hour into our walk, I spied a hummingbird ________________ above a large bush with tiny yellow flowers. I took a picture, thinking it was a personal ________________, since I usually forget to take my camera. I put my photo on a bird Web site, asking if anyone knew what kind it was. A couple of days later, I got an e-mail saying it was a rare Wolf-Neck Hummingbird and that no one had ever taken a photo of it before! I was able to ________________ something no one else had. It just goes to show, it never hurts to be in the right place at the right time!

Name ____

Read the selection. Complete the theme graphic organizer.

Detail

↓

Detail

↓

Detail

↓

Theme

Name ______________________________

As you read the poem, ask yourself what message the author wants you to understand.

Spelling Bee

Letters trip over each other
5 as they race to leave my mouth.
12 My tongue lines them up in order
19 as they march to the microphone:
25 A-S-
26 I am almost alone on the stage.
33 One last kid sags with his head
40 in his hands. He is mouthing
46 each letter as I say it:
52 C-E-N-
53 The hours I have spent on the floor
61 of my room with books
66 in my lap like wounded birds and cramping
74 wrists now seem worth it:
79 D-A-
80 There are lists of words
85 scribbled in my cursive and spelled
91 out in my parents' print
96 on top of dictionaries and thesauruses:
102 N-C-Y
103 There is applause and I smile.
109 I shake the seventh-grade boy's hand
115 and whisper, "I'll meet you back
121 here next year for a rematch."
127 A-S-C-E-N-D-A-N-C-Y

Name ____

A. Reread the passage and answer the questions.

1. What is this poem about?

____

____

____

2. What is the theme of this poem?

____

____

____

3. What in the poem lets you know what the theme is?

____

____

____

B. Work with a partner. Read the passage aloud. Pay attention to rate. Stop after one minute. Fill out the chart.

	Words Read	–	Number of Errors	=	Words Correct Score
First Read		–		=	
Second Read		–		=	

Name ______________________________

The Principal's Office

"Ms. Lee will see you now," the assistant said.
I swallowed hard and opened the door.
I've really done it, I thought.
As I stepped in, Ms. Lee looked up
And took an envelope from her desk.
"Daniel Birnbaum," she began.
"I just think that you ought to know"
—my heart was pounding in my chest—
"How proud we all are of your work."
Surprised, I saw the envelope read,
"District Youth Robotics Team."
"You made the district team!" she said.
I've really done it! I thought.

Answer the questions about the text.

1. What makes this text a narrative poem?

____

2. Briefly summarize the text's events.

____

____

____

3. What words repeat in the text?

____

4. How does the repetition show that the narrator's feelings have changed?

____

Name ______________________________

A **stanza** is two or more lines of poetry that together form a unit of the poem. Stanzas can be the same length and have a rhyme scheme, or vary in length and not rhyme.

Repetition is the use of repeated words and phrases in a poem. Poets use repetition for rhythmic effect and emphasis.

Read the lines of the narrative poem below. Then answer the questions.

Letters trip over each other
as they race to leave my mouth.
My tongue lines them up in order
as they march to the microphone:
A-S-

I am almost alone on the stage.
One last kid sags with his head
in his hands. He is mouthing
each letter as I say it:
C-E-N-

1. **Are there stanzas in this part of the poem? If so, how many and how many lines does each have?**

____

2. **What kind of repetition is in this poem? How does it affect the poem?**

____

____

____

3. **Write another stanza for this poem that includes the same structure and repetition.**

____

____

____

____

____

Name ____

Read each passage. Each word in bold has a different connotation in the poem than its usual denotation. Explain the connotation on the lines.

1. Letters **trip** over each other as they race to leave my mouth.

____

____

2. One last kid **sags** with his head in his hands. He is mouthing each word as I say it:

____

____

3. My tongue lines them up in order as they **march** to the microphone:

____

____

Name ______________________________

A. Read each sentence. Underline the word or words with the variant vowel /ô/ found in *hawk*. Then sort the words by their spellings in the chart below.

1. I love to eat strawberry shortcake.

2. The cat stalked the mouse in the yard.

3. I thought you might like to see the water at the beach.

4. The lady altered her shawl around her shoulders.

al	aw	wa	ough
5. ____________	7. ____________	9. ____________	10. ____________
6. ____________	8. ____________		

B. Circle the correct word in parentheses to complete each sentence. Use a dictionary to help you if necessary.

1. Did you (chose, choose) the red skateboard or the black one?

2. (Their, They're) waiting for us at the restaurant already.

3. I need some (advise, advice) about how to prepare for this test.

4. The baseball crashed (through, threw) the bedroom window.

5. I have (to, two) pairs of sneakers that I wear.

Name ______________________________

A. Read the draft model. Use the questions that follow the draft to help you think about what sensory details you can add.

Draft Model

I was nervous.
I waited to hear the election results.
The loudspeaker came on.
I was excited when I heard the principal say my name.

1. **What sensory details would better describe the speaker's nervousness in the first line?**

2. **What sensory details would more clearly show how the speaker "waited" to hear the election results?**

3. **What does the loudspeaker sound like to the speaker?**

4. **What sensory details would better describe the speaker's excitement in the last line?**

B. Now revise the draft by adding sensory details to help readers feel what the narrator is feeling.

____

____

____

____

____

____

Name ______________________________

Alex wrote the stanzas below using text evidence from two different sources to respond to the prompt: *Write a narrative poem about taking a math test. Use sensory language and figurative language.*

Math Victory

Test day, it's here–I am ready, I know it.
Desk lids slamming, papers rustling
Classmates hurry to get ready.

All of a sudden, my heart pounds like a drum.
Oh no...my palms feel cold and clammy.
Do I remember my times tables? Fractions?

But wait–I studied, I practiced–I have this.
Calmly and easily I glide through each problem
A smile on my face–I was ready, I knew it!

Reread the passage. Follow the directions below.

1. **Circle** an example of sensory language in the first stanza.

2. **Underline** a simile that Alex uses.

3. **Draw a box** around an example of sensory language that shows how the narrator feels.

4. **Write** a pronoun that Alex uses that's a homophone of its.

____

Name ____

bouquet	encircle	fussy	sparkles
emotion	express	portraits	whirl

Finish each sentence using the vocabulary word provided.

1. **(bouquet)** On Mother's Day ______________________________

____.

2. **(emotion)** Watching the sad movie ______________________________

____.

3. **(encircle)** When we play the game in the school yard, ______________

____.

4. **(express)** Some artists I know ______________________________

____.

5. **(fussy)** Whenever we go shopping, ______________________________

____.

6. **(portraits)** At the art museum ______________________________

____.

7. **(sparkles)** When I am in art class, ______________________________

____.

8. **(whirl)** I saw the couple on the dance floor ______________________

____.

Name ______________________________

Read the selection. Complete the problem and solution graphic organizer.

Characters

Setting

Problem

Event

Solution

Name ____

Read the passage. Use the visualize strategy to help you understand the story.

The Stray Dog

Kwan was in his neighborhood, walking home from the bus stop,
11 when a medium-sized dog came running up to him. It was a shaggy
24 white dog with orange spots and floppy ears and looked as if it didn't
38 belong to anybody. Kwan bent down for a closer look. He didn't
50 recognize the animal from any of the families in the neighborhood.
61 The dog was a big fluffy ball of dirt and had no tags, so there was
77 little doubt. The dog was a stray. Kwan wondered what he should do.
90 Kwan walked the rest of the way to his house, the dog following
103 behind him. When Kwan reached his front door, he picked up the dog
116 and walked inside. The dog wagged his tail frantically with pleasure
127 at being held. He felt like a huge sack of marbles in Kwan's arms
141 as Kwan carried him into the kitchen. His father was there pouring
153 orange juice into a glass. He took one look at Kwan and the dog and
168 nearly dropped the carton of juice.
174 "You can't keep it, Kwan," his father said. "I've already explained
185 to you that we don't have the time or space for a dog."
198 "I know, Dad," said Kwan, putting the dog down on the floor. "But
211 he's definitely a stray, and I really want to help him." The dog ran
225 over to the kitchen door where Kwan's dad kept a pair of running
238 shoes. He took both shoes in his mouth and ran back over to Kwan
252 and plopped the shoes down in front of him. The dog sat there with
266 his tongue hanging out, wagging his tail. Just then, Kwan's mom
277 walked in.

Name ____

"I guess he likes shoes," she said, smiling. "Why don't you take him to Uncle Bae's and see if he wants the dog?" She looked at Kwan pointedly and said, "He gets so few visitors."

"Okay, okay. I'll go see Uncle Bae," said Kwan. He grabbed an old belt from the closet to use for a leash and walked out the door.

Uncle Bae was Kwan's least favorite relative, mainly because he was a real grump. He was about as warm as a block of ice. As a young man, Uncle Bae had fought in the army and had his vision severely damaged so that now he could barely see.

"Come in!" his uncle called when Kwan rang the bell. Kwan walked into the living room with the dog, saying, "Hi, Uncle Bae. It's me, Kwan." His uncle was sitting in an easy chair.

"This stray dog followed me home this afternoon and Mom and Dad said I couldn't keep it," Kwan announced. "We thought you might like to keep him."

"What am I going to do with a dog?" said Uncle Bae angrily. "Get him away. But first, go get my shoes. They're in my bedroom."

Kwan smiled knowingly at the dog. He walked the dog into Uncle Bae's bedroom and brought him over to a pair of loafers. The dog grabbed the shoes in his mouth and ran back into the living room. He plopped the loafers right in Uncle Bae's lap. Uncle Bae's face lit up like the sun. It was the first time in a long time that Kwan saw his Uncle Bae smile. Uncle Bae looked at Kwan and said, "What should I name him?"

Name ______________________________

A. Reread the passage and answer the questions.

1. What is the main problem Kwan faces in the story?

____

____

____

2. What is Kwan's mother's suggestion?

____

____

3. What is Uncle Bae's first reaction to the dog?

____

4. What is the solution to Kwan's problem?

____

____

B. Work with a partner. Read the passage aloud. Pay attention to expression. Stop after one minute. Fill out the chart.

	Words Read	–	Number of Errors	=	Words Correct Score
First Read		–		=	
Second Read		–		=	

Name ____________________

A Change of Heart

"I'm just plain sick of helping Eric with reading," Jen told her father after school one day. "Sometimes he can be a real brat."

"Well," said Jen's father with a knowing smile, "before you quit, look in your room."

Jen went into her room and there on her bed was a little handmade book. It was titled "Best Sister." It was about a boy who gets an "A" in reading and thanks his sister for her help. Jen went to her father. "Maybe I'll read this book with Eric next," she said with a smile.

Answer the questions about the text.

1. How can you tell this is realistic fiction?

____

____

2. How are the characters in this text like characters from real life?

____

____

3. How does the author foreshadow that Jen will change her mind?

____

____

4. How does Jen feel about reading to her brother at the end of the text?

____

____

Name ____

Read each passage. Find and underline the simile or metaphor. Then identify what is being compared and if it is a simile or a metaphor.

1. Kwan bent down for a closer look. He didn't recognize the animal from any of the families in the neighborhood. The dog was a big fluffy ball of dirt and had no tags, so there was little doubt. The dog was a stray.

   Simile or metaphor? ____________________

   What is being compared? ____________________

   ____

2. Uncle Bae was Kwan's least favorite relative, mainly because he was a real grump. He was about as warm as a block of ice.

   Simile or metaphor? ____________________

   What is being compared? ____________________

   ____

3. He plopped the loafers right in Uncle Bae's lap. Uncle Bae's face lit up like the sun. It was the first time in a long time that Kwan saw his Uncle Bae smile.

   Simile or metaphor? ____________________

   What is being compared? ____________________

   ____

Name ____

A. Read each sentence. Underline the word that has two closed syllables. Write the word on the line and divide the syllables with a slanted line (/).

1. I am a member of the chess club at school. __________
2. The blanket is on top of the sofa. __________
3. The student dug a fossil out of the sand. __________
4. The child is going to get the plastic toy. __________
5. There is a lot of traffic at this time on Friday. __________

B. Read the definitions in the box below. Write the prefix and the root on the lines. Then write the meaning of the prefix on the line below each word.

> The Latin prefix *extra-* means "outside" or "beyond."
>
> The Latin prefix *inter-* means "between."

1. extracurricular ______________ ______________

   Prefix Meaning: ______________

2. interstate ______________ ______________

   Prefix Meaning: ______________

3. intermission ______________ ______________

   Prefix Meaning: ______________

4. extraordinary ______________ ______________

   Prefix Meaning: ______________

Name ______________________________

A. Read the draft model. Use the questions that follow the draft to help you think about how you can grab the reader's attention with a strong beginning.

Draft Model

Dad and I always help each other. Sometimes I help Dad in the kitchen. Other times, Dad helps me work on my bike or finish my homework.

1. How does the narrator help Dad in the kitchen?
2. How does Dad help with the bike?
3. How does Dad help with homework?
4. What opening sentence would introduce the topic and grab the reader's attention?

B. Now revise the draft by adding a strong beginning that introduces the topic clearly.

____

____

____

____

____

____

____

Name ______________________________

Imani wrote the letter below using text evidence from two different stories to answer the prompt: ***Write a letter from Luisa to Jana telling her how she felt when she heard how Jana helped the Ali family.***

Dear Jana,

I heard that you helped your friend's family who lost everything. It is so sad that the fire destroyed their home, but at least everyone is unhurt. Your plan to help was brilliant!

Last week, I organized a surprise birthday party for my mother. It was a dance party. Her fellow workers and customers all helped me. She was really surprised and was so happy that she even danced again. Mama has not danced in years. Yet, I feel that the happiness and excitement I gave my mother cannot compare to the generosity and kindness that you showed for Yasmin. The short poem you wrote helped your classmates understand what happened to Yasmin's family. I heard you collected not just clothes, but money, books, and a game player.

After hearing what you did for Yasmin, I know that she would do the same for you. I hope one day to have a friend as kind as you are.

Your friend,

Luisa

Reread the passage. Follow the directions below.

1. **Draw a circle** around the sentence in the opening that makes you want to read more about what Jana did for Yasmin.

2. **Underline** an inference that Luisa makes about Yasmin.

3. **Draw a box around** a detail that shows you Mama was happy.

4. **Write** an example from the letter of an adjective that modifies a noun.

____

Name ______________________________

territories	withered	plunging	settlement
scoffed	prospector	topple	shrivel

Use the context clues in each sentence to help you decide which vocabulary word fits best in the blank.

At school Belinda learned about Nellie Cashman, a famous ______________ who explored Alaska for gold. Belinda was inspired. Nellie had left her home to explore ______________ like Alaska and other large regions to look for gold.

"I'm going to be like Nellie Cashman," she told her sister, Jane.

Jane just ______________, mocking her sister. "Sure, like you're actually going to find something! You'll get lost out in the sun and ______________ up like a raisin!"

"I'll find something. Just you wait and see," said Belinda. She knew she could find minerals just like Nellie. It might not be gold she'd find, but she didn't plan on becoming dried up and ______________ in the sun like Jane thought she would.

Belinda and her family lived in an area that had woods, rivers, and streams. She felt that the ______________ where Nellie lived must have been almost the same. *Where would Nellie have looked?* Belinda asked herself. There was a small stream behind the house. Belinda remembered that people in Alaska found gold in streams and rivers. "I'll look there first!"

Belinda walked along the bank of the stream. Suddenly something in the shallow water caught her eye. She had to get down there and grab it. "Maybe it's gold!" Since the bank was steep, she walked carefully so she wouldn't ______________ over. The last thing she wanted was to go ______________ or diving into the cold stream.

Belinda made it to the stream and saw what was shining in the water. It was three shiny quarters sitting on the rocks and sand. Belinda swiped them up and put them in her pocket. "Well," she said as she climbed the bank, "it's not gold. But it's a good start!"

Name ____

Read the selection. Complete the cause-and-effect graphic organizer.

Cause	→	Effect
	→	
	→	
	→	
	→	

Name ____

Read the passage. Use the visualize strategy to make sure you understand what you read.

Working on the Weather

Now, back in the days of wagon trains and gold rushes, many
12 people were leaving the Midwest to live in California. They had heard
24 the weather was beautiful the whole year. The soil never got too dry.
37 They thought they could plant crops and never worry they would die
49 from the heat.

52 The summer of 1849 was so hot that even now in the Midwest,
65 150 years later, it is called the Great Heat. To add to the troubles, at the
81 beginning of September, it began to rain. It rained for the next month
94 straight! The problem was that when the rain got close to the ground,
107 the heat turned it to steam.

113 The steam did cool enough to turn into fog, though. The country
125 was covered in fog. The fog was so thick that ranchers could not see
139 to give their animals water. It didn't matter, though. The animals just
151 drank the fog right out of the air! Farmers weren't so happy, however.
164 The sun couldn't get through. The seeds didn't know which way was
176 up. They grew down into the ground!

183 Febold Feboldson decided to fix things when it came to the
194 weather. He ordered some fog scissors from London. They know their
205 fog. Unfortunately, the English sent them on a slow boat. Febold didn't
217 get the scissors until Thanksgiving.

Name ______________________________

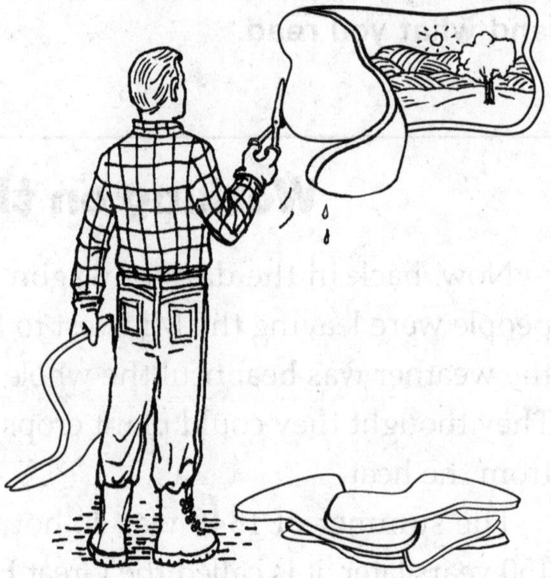

Febold finally got to work. He cut the fog out of the air in strips. He laid them down along the roads. That way they wouldn't drown the fields. After a while, the dust covered the roads. You couldn't even tell where Febold buried the fog. Everyone was excited at the time. However, many mail carriers in the middle of the country have whispered Febold's name in anger ever since. Every spring, even today, when it rains or thaws, the fog comes leaking out of the ground. It turns country roads into rivers of mud!

There's also another problem here in the Midwest. Sometimes there is just not enough rain. The next year, in 1850, there was a terrible drought. The sun shone for weeks. There were no clouds to cover the people in Nebraska.

Febold was annoyed, because he loved fishing. It was too sunny and hot to sit and wait for the fish to bite. So he decided to make some rain fall.

He collected all the wood and dry grass he could find. Then he went from lake to lake. He was building the biggest bonfires you've ever seen. He thought if he could get the fires really hot, they'd make the water in the lakes evaporate and form clouds. Soon there were many clouds in the sky from all the water rising out of the lakes. They bumped into each other and the rain began to fall!

Once Febold started the rain, it rained regularly again. The only problem was that the people on the plains had nowhere to swim, since there was no water in the lakes!

Name ______________________________

A. Reread the passage and answer the questions.

1. What happened when the rain got close to the ground during the Great Heat?

____

____

2. Why did the seeds grow down into the ground?

____

____

3. According to the third paragraph on the second page of the passage, what caused Febold to try to make some rain fall?

____

____

4. What was one effect of Febold making rain?

____

____

B. Work with a partner. Read the passage aloud. Pay attention to intonation and phrasing. Stop after one minute. Fill out the chart.

	Words Read	–	Number of Errors	=	Words Correct Score
First Read		–		=	
Second Read		–		=	

Name Marin

The Mighty John Henry

When Americans started moving west, the country needed a railroad for faster travel. John Henry worked to help build that railroad. He was the strongest man to ever live.

The railroad needed to pass through Big Bend Mountain, and the boss wanted to use a powered drill to get through the rock. But that drill would put John Henry out of work! So John Henry challenged the mechanical drill to a digging competition. With two twenty-pound hammers in each hand, John Henry dug 15 feet in 35 minutes. He beat the machine and saved the day!

Answer the questions about the text.

1. How can you tell this is a tall tale?

I can tell because it has exageration.

2. What is one example of hyperbole in the text?

One hyperbole is that he dug d 15 feet in 35 minutes.

3. In what way is John Henry a larger-than-life hero?

He is larger-than-life hero because he did what a mushin can't do.

4. Why does the author include details about how far John Henry and the machine dug?

The author included this because he Wanted to tell us he is the strogest man.

Name ____

Read each sentence below. Underline the context clues that help you understand the meaning of each homograph in bold. Then write the correct definition of the homograph on the line.

1. Now, back in the days of wagon trains and gold rushes, many people were leaving the Midwest to **live** in California.

____

2. To add to the troubles, at the beginning of **fall**, it began to rain.

____

3. The problem was that when the rain got **close** to the ground, the heat turned it to steam.

____

4. They grew down into the **ground**!

____

5. He was **building** the biggest bonfires you've ever seen.

____

- rivers, montans
- 2,000 miles
- a lot of pain [redacted]
- dust stormes
-
-
-
-

Name ____

A. Read the words below. Use a slanted line (/) to divide each word into its syllables. On the line, write whether the first syllable is "open" or "closed."

1. prevent ____________________

2. famous ____________________

3. ribbon ____________________

4. bookend ____________________

5. cider ____________________

6. vacancy ____________________

B. Draw a line to match each singular noun with its correct plural rule. Then write the plural form of the noun on the line.

1. hoof	change middle vowels	____________
2. woman	change middle vowels and consonant	____________
3. tooth	make no change	____________
4. mouse	change ending to *-ves*	____________
5. deer	change ending to *-en*	____________

Name ____

A. Read the draft model. Use the questions that follow the draft to help you think about what sentence types you can use.

Draft Model

Tall tales teach about life. Tall tales entertain. My grandmother tells me tall tales. I think tall tales are clever and fun to read, and I love tall tales.

1. How could you combine the first two sentences to make one longer sentence?
2. How could you rewrite the third sentence to provide more detail?
3. How could you rewrite the last sentence as two sentences to strengthen the narrator's final point?

B. Now revise the draft by using different types of sentences to make it more interesting to read.

____

____

____

____

____

____

____

____

Name ______________________________

Gabriel used text evidence from two different sources to respond to the prompt: *Add an event to* Apples to Oregon. *Describe another challenge Delicious overcomes. Use one of the challenges described in* "Westward Bound: Settling the American West."

The snow was up to my eyeballs. Daddy and I were wading through it, trying to get through the mountain pass. Suddenly, the sound of a woman's wild laughter swirled through the snowflakes. It was that nasty, mean-spirited Old Woman Winter!

Daddy said, "I'm going to need your help, Delicious." Then he vanished.

The cold voice of Old Woman Winter cackled in my ear. "You beat Jack Frost, but you'll never beat me! Say good-bye to your father and his precious fruit trees!"

There's no call for someone to be so mean. "Old Woman Winter, you have messed with the wrong gal!"

I jumped on a snowflake and rode it right up to Old Woman Winter. I grabbed her long icy hair and swung her around and around. When I let go, she went flying clean up to Canada.

I found Daddy, and we crossed the mountains without any more trouble.

Reread the passage. Follow the directions below.

1. **Circle** an example of hyperbole that Gabriel uses.

2. **Draw a box** around two sentences of different lengths that are next to each other.

3. **Underline** what Delicious did after she let go of Old Woman Winter.

4. **Write** two articles on the line that Gabriel uses in his story.

____

Name ______________________________

mischief	procedure	dizzy	politician
genuine	nowadays	hilarious	experiment

Use a word from the box to answer each question. Then use the word in a sentence.

1. How can a spinning ride at the playground make you feel? ____________

____

2. What is another word for *real*? ____________

____

3. What word can be used to compare something with the past? ____________

____

4. What might a scientist use as a test to discover something? ____________

____

5. What would you call a person who seeks public office? ____________

____

6. How might you describe your favorite comedian on television? ____________

____

7. What can someone create if they cause harm or trouble? ____________

____

8. How would you describe a series of steps used to accomplish an action?

____

____

Name ______________________________

Read the selection. Complete the problem and solution graphic organizer.

Problem	**Solution**

Name ______________________________

Read the passage. Use the summarize strategy to find the most important ideas in the passage.

Breaking the Silence

American Sign Language is used by millions of people. The
10 hearing impaired have used it for years. A young science student
21 named José Hernández-Rebollar noticed that few people who could
30 hear knew ASL. They couldn't communicate with the hearing
39 impaired. He set out to make a new tool that would help solve this
53 problem. With it, he also saw a new way for the hearing impaired to
67 communicate.

68 **Early Years**

70 Hernández-Rebollar worked as an engineer in his native Mexico.
79 He even had a part in making what became the largest telescope in
92 the world!
94 In 1998, he received a grant to study in the United States. He chose
108 to get his Ph.D. degree at George Washington University, where he
119 studied electrical engineering. In 2000, he began work on his school
130 project. It was an idea for a new glove.

139 **His Invention**

141 Hernández-Rebollar called his tool the AcceleGlove. What was
149 the logic? People used their hands to sign. The glove could turn sign
162 language into spoken or printed words.
168 This process of turning movement into voice involves many steps.
178 It starts when the glove is put on the hand and strapped to the arm.
193 The glove sends signals made by where and how the hand and wrist
206 move. The glove compares where the wrist and hand are to where the
219 body is.

Name ______________________________

A computer receives the signals. It then categorizes and links the hand movement with the correct word. An automatic computer voice then says the word.

Dr. Hernández-Rebollar's AcceleGlove helps hearing and non-hearing people communicate.

Uses for the Glove

The AcceleGlove can do many things. It can be helpful when something is urgent. People can exchange words quickly. It can also be used to teach ASL or for other forms of sign language.

The glove can translate ASL into Spanish as well as English. This can help people who move to this country. There is hope that one day the glove will help create one common sign language. Each country would not need its own.

Also, the total number of words that the glove knows will increase as more studies are done. There will be fewer mistakes.

There are other uses for the glove for people who can hear. People in the armed forces use a communication technique that involves silent gestures out in the field. The glove can help them send wireless notes back and forth. They would only need to move their hands.

It can also be used for fun in the online world of games. To move within a video game or direct a game with the glove are new ways a person can play.

Hernández-Rebollar's AcceleGlove has a wide range of uses. It is a tool that could end up meeting the needs of the hearing and non-hearing alike.

Name ____

A. Reread the passage and answer the questions.

1. What problem is presented in paragraph 1?

____

____

2. What solution is presented to the problem in paragraph 1?

____

____

3. What is another example of a possible problem and its solution in paragraph 8?

____

____

____

____

B. Work with a partner. Read the passage aloud. Pay attention to rate and accuracy. Stop after one minute. Fill out the chart.

	Words Read	–	Number of Errors	=	Words Correct Score
First Read		–		=	
Second Read		–		=	

Name ______________________________

Thomas Edison

Thomas Edison was one of the world's greatest inventors. He was born in 1847 in Milan, Ohio. As a child, Edison was curious about the way things worked. Many of Edison's inventions led to machines that we still use today. In 1877, he invented the phonograph, which later became the record player. In 1879 he made a long-lasting light bulb. His Kinetograph of 1891 later became the movie camera.

Library of Congress, Prints and Photographs Division

Thomas Edison thought up over 1,000 inventions.

Answer the questions about the text.

1. How can you tell this text is a biography?

____

2. What text feature is included in this text?

____

3. How do the photo and caption help you understand the text better? What information do they give you?

____

____

4. In what order are the events of the text told?

____

____

Name ______________________________

Greek root	**Meaning**
tele	far
log	thought
mis	wrongly
auto	self
techn	art, skill

Read the sentences below. Then look at the Greek roots and their meanings above. Underline the word in each sentence that contains a Greek root and write the Greek root on the line. Then write the definition of the underlined word on the line.

1. He even had a part in making what became the largest telescope in the world!

____

2. What was the logic?

____

3. An automatic computer voice then says the word.

____

4. There will be fewer mistakes.

____

5. People in the armed forces use a communication technique that involves silent gestures out in the field.

____

Name ______________________________

A. Read each sentence. Underline the word with a vowel team syllable. On the line, write the letters that make the vowel team.

1. My trainer helped me practice for the game. __________
2. Is he giving a discount for this scratched item? __________
3. I will study to increase my chances of getting a better grade. __________
4. I will not reveal the secret of her amazing magic trick. __________
5. A baboon is an interesting type of animal. __________
6. The staircase rose endlessly to the sky. __________

B. Read the meanings of the roots. Draw a line to match the words with the same root. Then write the meaning of the root on the line.

The Greek root *scop* means "see." The Latin root *ped* means "foot."

The Greek root *bio* means "life." The Latin root *aud* means "listen."

The Greek root *photo* means "light."

1. autobiography	periscope	__________
2. pedestrian	telephoto	__________
3. telescope	pedal	__________
4. auditorium	biological	__________
5. photocopier	audible	__________

Name ______________________________

A. Read the draft model. Use the questions that follow the draft to help you use transitions to connect ideas.

Draft Model

Why is the smartphone the most important invention? It helps people stay connected. It allows people to look up information easily. You can use it to get directions. It is not just a phone—it is a tiny computer.

1. How many supporting sentences are there for this draft model?
2. Is there a logical flow from one idea to the next?
3. What transition words would fit well at the beginning of some of the supporting sentences?

B. Now revise the draft by adding transitions to move smoothly from one idea to another.

____

____

____

____

____

____

____

____

Name ______________________________

Brady wrote the paragraphs below using text evidence from two different sources to answer the prompt: *How did Ben Franklin use electrical energy and how is it used today?*

In *How Ben Franklin Stole the Lightning*, Franklin believed that lightning was electricity, and he proved it. His kite experiment showed that electricity moves through wire. At the time, lightning strikes were causing a lot of fires. So Franklin invented the lightning rod, which controlled electricity by channeling the electricity in lightning safely into the ground.

Next, electricity was distributed through wires, and modern life came to depend on it. "Energy is Everywhere" tells us that electricity is an "energy carrier," because it's created from one form of energy, such as fossil fuels, and produces another form of energy, such as light from a light bulb. First, the electrical energy is created in power plants and then travels to homes and factories through wires. When people "plug into it," the electrical energy produces other types of energy. Electricity is easier to use now than it was in Franklin's time.

Reread the passage. Follow the directions below.

1. **Draw a circle** around a concrete word that describes how Franklin controlled electricity.

2. **Underline** a transition word that connects the two paragraphs.

3. **Draw a box around** an example that supports the idea that electricity is created from one form of energy.

4. **Write** a sentence from the essay that uses an adjective that compares.

____

Name ______________________________

cling	humid	magnify	mingle
microscope	dissolves	typical	gritty

Finish each sentence using the vocabulary word provided.

1. **(gritty)** After a day at the beach, ______________________________

______________________________.

2. **(humid)** I was not used to ______________________________

______________________________.

3. **(typical)** Even though she was not ______________________________

______________________________.

4. **(microscope)** In order to see the ______________________________

______________________________.

5. **(dissolves)** If you add water ______________________________

______________________________.

6. **(magnify)** His glasses ______________________________

______________________________.

7. **(cling)** In the tall tree ______________________________

______________________________.

8. **(mingle)** At the school party ______________________________

______________________________.

Name ______________________________

Read the selection. Complete the sequence graphic organizer.

Name ______________________________

Read the passage. Use the summarize strategy to make sure you understand the text.

At Your Fingertips

What makes you different? Is it your hair or is it your name? Is
14 it the shape of your eyes and nose? All of these may be important.
28 However, there is one thing that truly sets you apart from everyone:
40 your fingerprints. You might not think of your fingerprints as part
51 of your identity. But they have replaced other uncertain methods of
62 identification. If you look closely, you can see that fingerprinting
72 is a reliable way of identifying people.
79 As we age, our looks change. Our hair and height may change and
92 even our face may change shape. There is one thing that stays the
105 same: our fingerprints. Unless you injure your fingertips, your prints
115 will be the same for your entire life, not just part of it. You will have
131 the same prints as an adult that you did as a child.
143 No two people are known to have the same prints. A quick look at
157 your fingertips might not prove much. Take a detailed look, though.
168 There are swirls and ridges. All of those shapes are specific to you.
181 The shapes you see are not the same for anyone else. Your prints are
195 unique. This is how they help to identify people. It took many years
208 for us to know the importance of fingerprints, though.

Name ______________________________

In 1858, Sir William Herschel of England had people sign papers with handprints. He then used fingerprints. The more fingerprints he saw, the more he noticed how no prints were the same. It seemed no two prints were identical. He saw that prints might be used to identify people.

In 1892, scientist Sir Francis Galton wrote a book about prints. He proved that they do not alter during a person's life. They remain the same. He said that it was not likely for two people to have the same prints. The odds of two people having the same prints were 1 in 64 billion!

Galton's proof was used by police to help solve crimes. In 1901, the London police began using prints to find people. They found this was the best way. They could be sure they had found the right person to arrest. In 1903, the New York State Prison system began using prints to identify criminals, too.

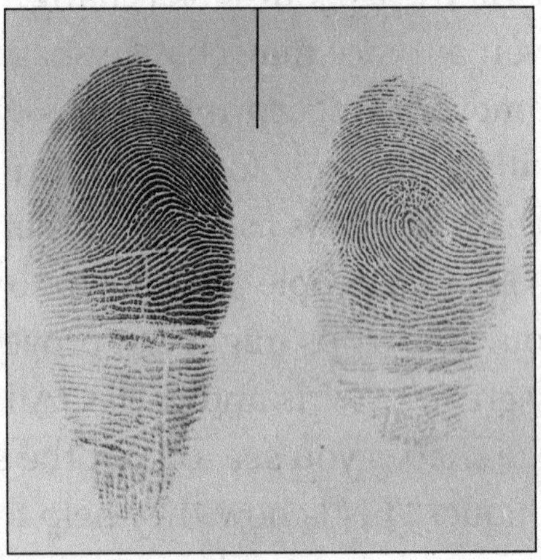
Stockbyte/Getty Images

Every fingerprint has a unique set of swirls and ridges.

Fingerprints can be used for more than identifying criminals. Fingerprints have since been used for identification by the U.S. Navy, the U.S. Marine Corps, and the F.B.I. Fingerprint scans can also act as a "key" to unlock a door or open files on a computer. Since they are unique, fingerprints are a sure way of keeping certain offices and files safe. Did you know that children are often fingerprinted to keep them from getting lost?

The importance of fingerprints has proved to be a great discovery. Whether used to sign papers, identify criminals, or unlock doors, prints are a reliable way to identify people. When we want to know who people are, we can look at their faces or ask their names. If we want to be sure, we have to look closely at the swirls and ridges on their fingertips.

Name ______________________________

A. Reread the passage and answer the questions.

1. What did Sir William Herschel discover in 1858?

____

____

____

2. According to the text, what was the next discovery after Herschel's?

____

____

____

3. How do you know that the information in the text is presented in time order?

____

____

____

B. Work with a partner. Read the passage aloud. Pay attention to rate. Stop after one minute. Fill out the chart.

	Words Read	–	Number of Errors	=	Words Correct Score
First Read		–		=	
Second Read		–		=	

Name ______________________________

Scott Aldrich's Micro Art

Scott Aldrich uses microscopes and light to make art. Aldrich was trained as a chemist. He often used microscopes to look at chemicals. The shapes he saw inspired his art. Aldrich uses light filters. The filters allow certain colors to pass through chemicals. Then he takes pictures of the substances using a camera with a built-in microscope. The pictures often look like familiar objects and animals!

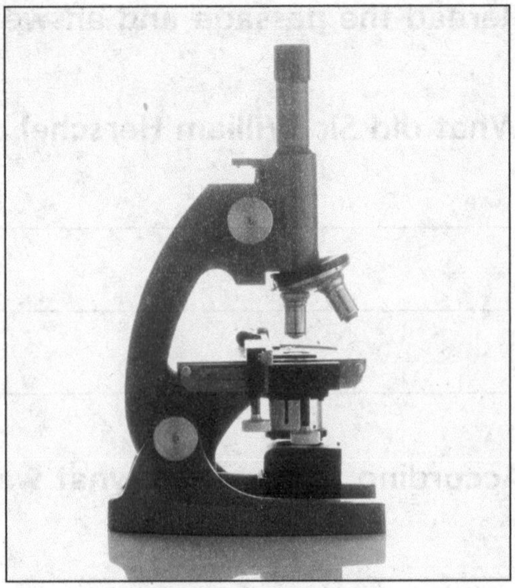

Siri Stafford

In his photography, Aldrich reveals the world as seen through a microscope.

Answer the questions about the text.

1. How do you know this is an expository text?

____

2. What text features does the text include?

____

3. What does the photograph show? How does it add to the text?

____

____

4. What information does the caption give you?

____

____

Name ______________________________

A. Draw lines to match each word in Column 1 with an antonym in Column 2.

Column 1	**Column 2**
1. identical	a. simple
2. reliable	b. maintain
3. entire	c. different
4. alter	d. part
5. specific	e. general
6. detailed	f. unsteady

B. Rewrite each sentence below using an antonym for the underlined word.

1. We stayed to watch the <u>entire</u> movie.

____

2. My mother did <u>not alter</u> the soup recipe.

____

3. The math lesson was so <u>detailed</u> that I had to take notes.

____

Name ________________________________

A. Read each sentence. Underline any words that have *r*-controlled vowel syllables. Then circle the letters that make the *r*-controlled vowel syllable.

1. The popular singer was going to play a show in my town.

2. When I enter the shop, I always notice a strange odor.

3. That object can be a danger to people walking along the harbor.

4. My daughter loves to ride up and down on the elevator.

5. I prefer real chili peppers to the powder that is available.

6. He could not pull up his coat zipper because it was broken.

B. Circle the correct word in parentheses to complete each sentence. Use a dictionary to help you if necessary.

1. My sister is better at math (then, than) my brother.

2. Do you understand the (moral, morale) of the story?

3. Please (lay, lie) the book down on the table.

4. I immediately saw the (affect, effect) of the sun on my skin.

5. The wind caused the (lose, loose) tile to fall from the rooftop.

Name ______________________________

A. Read the draft model. Use the questions that follow the draft to help you use a formal voice.

Draft Model

The teacher uses this thing a lot. You can't pick it up, but you can write all over it. It gets totally dusty with chalk. It's not a super cool thing, but it does the job.

1. What are some examples of conversational language in the first sentence?

2. What formal language can be used to replace these words in the first sentence?

3. How will formal language improve the draft model?

4. Where else in the draft model can formal language be used to replace conversational words or slang?

B. Now revise the draft by adding words and phrases that show a formal voice.

____

____

____

____

____

____

____

Name ______________________________

Delia used text evidence from two different sources to answer the prompt: ***How do* A Drop of Water *and* "The Incredible Shrinking Potion" *convince readers to look closely at something?***

The authors of *A Drop of Water* and "The Incredible Shrinking Potion" convince readers that things look different when they are magnified. We see amazing details we had not seen before.

A Drop of Water is an informative text. The author uses words and photos to show how and why water changes. For example, he includes photos of a snowflake magnified to 60 times its actual size. He also shows sleet that is 15 times its actual size. This helps readers see the most amazing details they could not see on their own.

In the story, "The Incredible Shrinking Potion," Isabel and Mariela have to look at the world in a different way when they shrink themselves to save their classmates. Now it is as though everything in their world is magnified because they are so small. For example, Isabel has to avoid the wide wooden grooves on the table. She never even noticed them when she was her normal height. Both authors manage to convince readers that it is important to take a closer look when things are magnified.

Reread the passage. Follow the directions below.

1. **Underline** Delia's opinion in the first paragraph.

2. **Draw a box** around an example Delia includes to support her opinion.

3. Delia uses a formal voice, so she avoids using contractions. **Circle** an example of formal voice.

4. **Write** the example of how Delia uses *most* to compare.

____

Name ______________________________

uncover	era	tremendous	evidence
expedition	document	permanent	archaeology

Use a word from the box to answer each question. Then use the word in a sentence.

1. What is the scientific study of the way people lived in the past?

____

____

2. What word might be used to describe an elephant? ______________

____

3. What could a group of people looking for lions be called? ______________

____

4. What is important to have to convince people that you saw an alien? ________

____

5. What is another way to say you keep a record of something? ____________

____

6. What is something that is intended to last without change? ____________

____

7. What is another word for *disclose*? ______________________

____

8. What could the time period of the dinosaurs be considered? ____________

____

Name ______________________________

Read the selection. Complete the sequence graphic organizer.

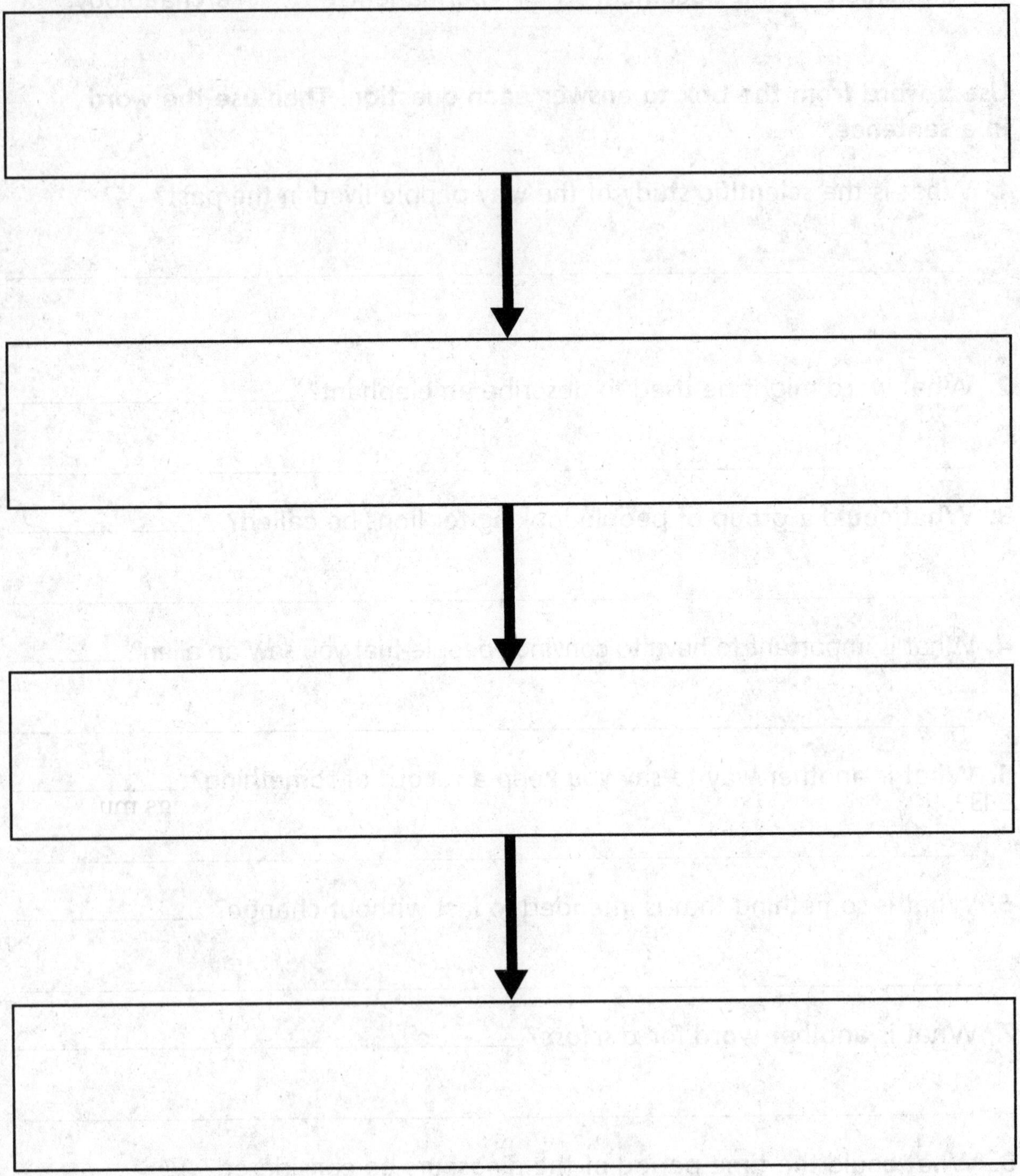

Name ______________________________

Read the passage. Use the summarize strategy to find the most important ideas in the passage.

Eastern Influence

The first Asian immigrants to enter the United States were from
11 China and some came as early as the 1700s. But most came looking
24 for gold in California in the mid-1800s. The Chinese brought their
35 culture. They also brought the skills to perform many jobs. Their
46 influence in those early years is still felt today.

55 **Culture and Adapting**

58 In 1848, word spread across the world that gold had been found in
71 the United States. The Gold Rush began in the West. Thousands of
83 people rushed to California dreaming of a better life. The Chinese
94 came as well.

97 The Chinese brought their culture to America. They had their own
108 language and belief systems to share. They shared their customs and
119 food with the West.

123 In the search for gold, it was every man for himself. At first the
137 Chinese had no trouble finding gold. But then, all good things must
149 come to an end. The people looking for gold increased. Gold became
161 harder to find. At last, the Chinese found themselves looking for other
173 ways to make money. They opened shops for work. They also ran
185 cleaning and laundry services.

189 **Sharing Skills**

191 Many of the Chinese that came were from farming areas in China.
203 In the 1850s, they used their skills in California. They grew food
215 close to home and sold it door-to-door. Citrus fruits, peanuts, and rice
227 were among the things they grew.

Name ____

The Chinese also helped to make California a good place for fishing. Many of the Chinese were experts. They fished for cod, flounder, and shark. They also took oysters and mussels from the water. They sold their food in local markets. They also salt-dried it and shipped it to other areas.

A Strong Work Ethic

The Chinese showed that hard work pays off. They played a vital role in the first transcontinental railroad in America. It was built from 1863 to 1869. It was the first railroad to connect the East and the West.

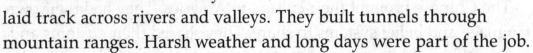

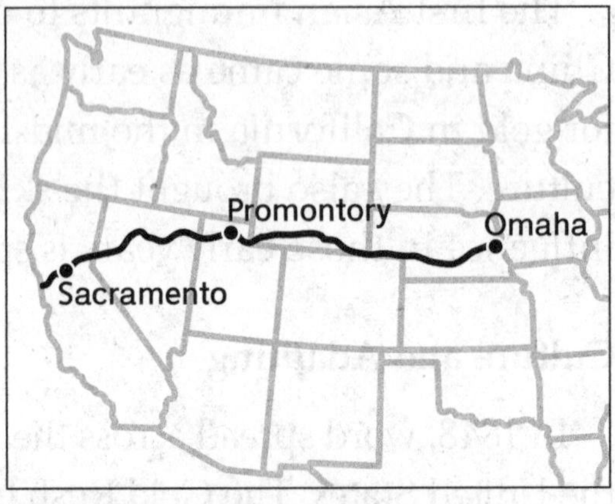

Chinese immigrants played an important role in the building of the first transcontinental railroad.

By 1868, most of the thousands of workers on the railroad were Chinese. They laid track across rivers and valleys. They built tunnels through mountain ranges. Harsh weather and long days were part of the job.

With the railroad came trade across the country. The West had crops that the East wanted. Farms grew in size and farmers were needed. The Chinese were called upon to help farm the land. Crops were then sent east.

The Chinese had a big influence on life in the West. They helped shape the country into what it is today.

A Different Kind of Medicine

Medicine and cures in the 1800s in America were not advanced. Rules for drugs were not set. The Chinese brought time-tested herbs for medicine. They had herbal treatments that had been around for thousands of years. Herbs from Asia are often still used today. People believe that they have little or no side effects.

Name ____

A. Reread the passage and answer the questions.

1. According to the sequence of the text, what happened first in 1848?

____

____

____

2. What important event happened later from 1863 to 1869?

____

____

____

3. How do you know that the information in the text is presented in time order?

____

____

____

B. Work with a partner. Read the passage aloud. Pay attention to rate and expression. Stop after one minute. Fill out the chart.

	Words Read	–	Number of Errors	=	Words Correct Score
First Read		–		=	
Second Read		–		=	

Name ____

A Visit to the Past

To learn more about early United States history, you should visit Pilgrim Memorial State Park in Plymouth, Massachusetts. This park is home to Plymouth Rock, where according to tradition the Pilgrims first set foot in the New World. A reconstruction of the *Mayflower*, the ship the Pilgrims sailed on, is docked nearby. Every year nearly one million people from all over the world come to see these symbols of America's past.

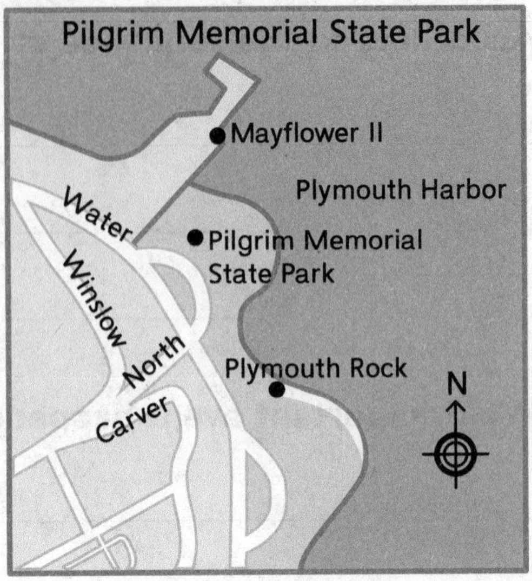

Answer the questions about the text.

1. How do you know this is an informational text?

____

2. What is the topic of the text?

____

3. What text feature is included? How does it add to the text?

____

____

4. How could visiting Plymouth help you learn about the past?

____

____

Name ____

Read each group of sentences below. Underline the context clues that help you understand the meaning of the proverb or adage in bold. Then write the meaning of the proverb or adage in bold.

1. In the search for gold, it was **every man for himself**. The people looking for gold increased. Gold became harder to find.

____

2. At first the Chinese had no trouble finding gold. But then, **all good things must come to an end**. At last, the Chinese found themselves looking for other ways to make money.

____

3. The Chinese showed that **hard work pays off**. They played a vital role in the first transcontinental railroad in America. They laid track across rivers and valleys. They built tunnels through mountain ranges.

____

4. People heard about gold being discovered in the United States. But **seeing is believing**. Immigrants came to the West from many countries to find out for themselves.

____

5. The Chinese fished for many types of fish for years. **Practice makes perfect**, and the Chinese became experts.

____

Name ______________________________

A. Read each sentence. Underline any words that end with a consonant + *le* syllable. Then circle the final syllable in the word.

1. My uncle plays the fiddle in a band.

2. A single pebble made me trip and hurt my ankle.

3. I do not want to tangle my hair in the buckle on this hat.

4. Do not cuddle with any of the animals in this jungle!

5. He had trouble cleaning the marble countertop.

6. I have a freckle on the bottom of my foot.

B. The Latin suffixes *-ible* and *-able* mean "can be done" or "the quality or state of" something. The Latin suffix *-ment* means "the state, action, or result of." Write the meaning of each word below.

1. wonderment ______________________________

2. convincible ______________________________

3. establishment ______________________________

4. punishable ______________________________

5. sellable ______________________________

6. permissible ______________________________

Name ______________________________

A. Read the draft model. Use the questions that follow the draft to help you think about how you can end an informational article with a strong concluding statement.

Draft Model

Thomas Edison was an American inventor. He invented over 1,000 different things. Because he invented the electric light bulb, I don't have to do my homework by candle light!

1. What main idea might the concluding statement sum up?

2. What might be other reasons Edison's invention of the electric light bulb was important?

3. What idea or detail would best sum up the writer's thoughts?

B. Now revise the draft by adding a strong concluding sentence that sums up the writer's thoughts.

____

____

____

____

____

____

____

Name ______________________________

Byron wrote the paragraphs below using text evidence from two different sources to respond to the prompt: *Compare and contrast some of the first attempts at settlements by colonists in America.*

Since the colonists of early America faced so many hardships, many of their attempts to settle here went from bad to worse. In "Rediscovering Our Spanish Beginnings," I learned that when Florida was first discovered it was hard to establish a colony there. Six attempts to settle in that area were unsuccessful because of harsh weather, dangerous animals, and soil that wouldn't grow European crops. The author says that St. Augustine was finally settled, but that the settlement became a target for enemy attack. It was forced to relocate many times over the next six years.

The colonists of Roanoke Island also left their settlement, but we don't know why. However, historians have some theories. These include disease, starvation, and being killed by hostile Native Americans. English colonists built a settlement off the coast of Maine, called "Popham," but it too did not survive.

Whether it was from enemy attacks, harsh weather, or starvation, these early settlements struggled to survive and very few did.

Reread the passage. Follow the directions below.

1. **Circle** one example of why early American settlements were unsuccessful.

2. **Draw a box** around the detail that tells how many attempts were made to settle Florida.

3. **Underline** one of the details that Byron gives for the disappearance of the Roanoke Island colony.

4. **Write** Byron's example of comparing with "bad" on the line below.

____

Name ____

intensity	forfeit	retreated	ancestors
endurance	irritating	despised	honor

Finish each sentence using the vocabulary word provided.

1. (intensity) During the football game, ______________________________

____.

2. (endurance) It is important for athletes ______________________________

____.

3. (forfeit) As a result of not having enough players, ____________________

____.

4. (irritating) When I'm watching a movie ______________________________

____.

5. (retreated) When it started to rain, ______________________________

____.

6. (despised) As a younger kid ______________________________

____.

7. (ancestors) The pictures on our walls ______________________________

____.

8. (honor) At the awards ceremony, ______________________________

____.

Name ______________________________

Read the selection. Complete the theme graphic organizer.

Detail

Detail

Detail

Theme

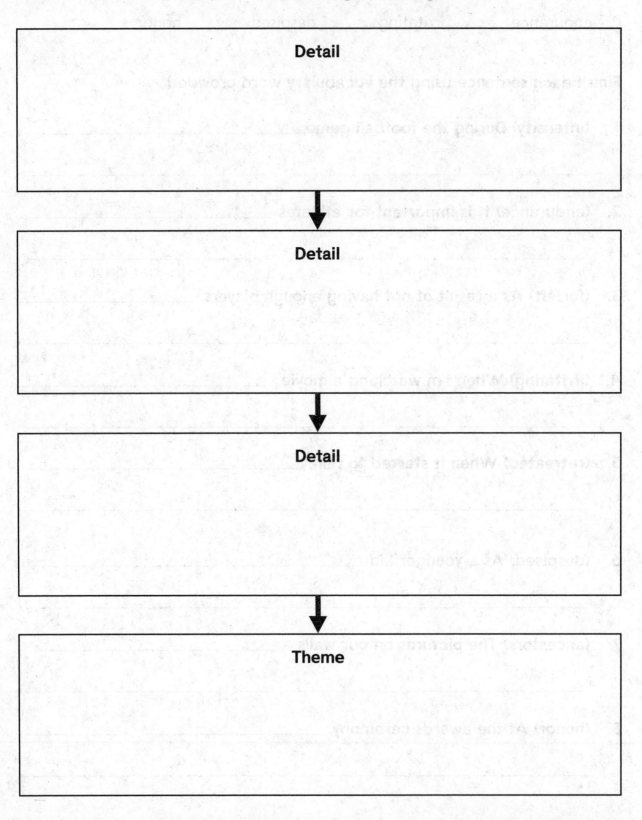

Name ______________________________

Read the passage. Use the reread strategy to understand difficult parts of the text.

The Generation Belt

Kanti snuck behind her village's circle of wigwams. One Algonquin
10 family was repairing their home with fresh birch bark strips. Kanti
21 stayed in the shadow of the trees until she reached the lake. She could
35 see her father's sleek canoe far off in the distance. He was fishing for
49 their dinner. Her cousins were splashing merrily near the shore and
60 waved to her. She stepped into the water.
68 "Kanti!" an irritated voice said.
73 Kanti felt her heart drop to her stomach. She was caught. Kanti's
85 mother walked quickly toward her. "Kanti, you know that your
95 grandmother is going to teach you today."
102 "It's so steamy outside. Why can't I swim with my cousins?"
113 she whined.
115 Her mother looked sympathetic, but firm. "Sometimes we have to
125 set aside play so we can learn. Come, I think you will like this lesson
140 better than you predict."
144 Kanti's grandmother looked dignified sitting cross-legged in the
152 center of their wigwam. Around her lay wide beaded belts of white
164 and purple with all kinds of vivid designs. In front of her was a loom
179 shaped like an archer's bow with a few rows of beads strung.
191 "Thanks for coming, Kanti." There was a mischievous glint in her
202 grandmother's eye. She held a few small purple beads. "Do you know
214 what these are?"
217 "That's easy, they're wampum." Sometimes Kanti would help
225 collect the quahog, or clams, the beads were made from.

Name ______________________________

"I actually meant, what do the beads stand for?" Kanti's grandmother said. "Here, let me show you."

She held out one of the most elaborate belts for Kanti to see. The purple beads made a pattern of triangles on the right side. On the left side, two figures stood holding hands next to a wigwam. "These people are your great-great grandmother and grandfather," she said. "They traveled over the mountains to find a place to settle." She traced the triangles with her fingers, stopping at one with the outline of a majestic bird hovering over it. "Your great-great grandmother saw an eagle that led them through the mountains." A circle at the edge of the mountains represented the lake that fed the village. "When they found a wide lake, they knew it would support many people. This is how our village began."

Despite herself, Kanti was drawn in by the story the belt portrayed. Suddenly, the belts' patterns jumped out at her, all holding adventures of their own. She looked at the loom with a scant five rows completed. "What story will this belt tell?" she asked.

"This belt will tell your story," her grandmother said. "I started it for you and you can continue to add to it as you grow." With that, her grandmother carefully stacked the belts and left.

Kanti immediately set to work, concentrating on finding just the right shades of purple wampum before stringing together rows. The purple beads became a figure about to leap into a calm lake. She couldn't wait for her cousins to come back so she could show them her new belt.

Name ______________________________

A. Reread the passage and answer the questions.

1. Why can't Kanti swim with her cousins?

____

____

____

2. What does Kanti learn about the belts?

____

____

____

3. What is the theme of this story?

____

____

____

B. Work with a partner. Read the passage aloud. Pay attention to rate and accuracy. Stop after one minute. Fill out the chart.

	Words Read	–	Number of Errors	=	Words Correct Score
First Read		–		=	
Second Read		–		=	

Name ____

A Roman Tradition

"Come help me pick flowers from the garden," Cornelia's mother called.

Cornelia got up and followed her mother outside. Their house stood on a hill outside the city of Rome, and from their garden they could look out over the empire's capital.

"What do we need the flowers for?" Cornelia asked.

"To decorate the *lararium*," her mother said. She turned and pointed to the house's courtyard. A small building stood in the corner. It looked like a tiny temple. Columns held up its triangular roof, and a group of small statues and oil lamps sat inside.

"Three times a month, we bring flowers and honey to the spirits of the household. That way they'll protect our house and our crops," she explained.

Answer the questions about the text.

1. How do you know this text is historical fiction?

____

____

2. What literary element is included in this piece of historical fiction?

____

3. Do you think the dialogue is fictional or historical?

____

4. What tradition does Cornelia's family have?

____

____

Name ____

Read each sentence below. For each word in bold, write the denotation on the line. Then write its connotation.

1. She could see her father's **sleek** canoe far off in the distance.

____

____

2. It's so **steamy** outside.

____

____

3. "Why can't I swim with my cousins?" she **whined**.

____

____

4. Kanti's grandmother looked **dignified** sitting cross-legged in the center of their wigwam.

____

____

5. She looked at the loom with a **scant** five rows completed.

____

____

Name ____

A. Read each sentence. Circle the word that ends with the same sound as *on* in *person*. Then sort the words in the chart below.

1. Today I am going to visit my cousin who lives in the city.

2. The group searched endlessly for the sunken treasure.

3. Did you know that a raisin is a grape that is partially dried out?

4. It was difficult to choose a gift, but I finally decided on the woven shirt.

5. The dinosaur skeleton at the museum was as big as a house!

-in	*-en*	*-on*
6. ______________	8. ______________	10. ______________
7. ______________	9. ______________	

B. Read the definitions for the prefixes below. Then read each word and circle the prefix. Write the meaning of the word based on the prefix. Use a dictionary to help you if necessary.

uni-, mono-	=	one	*deca-*	=	ten
bi-	=	two	*cent-*	=	hundred
tri-	=	three			

1. monotone ______________________________

2. bimonthly ______________________________

3. centimeter ______________________________

4. unicolor ______________________________

Name ____

A. Read the draft model. Use the questions that follow the draft to help you think about what strong words you can add.

Draft Model

Every winter, my family has "beach day" at home. We fill a plastic pool with sand and make sand castles. We listen to music and dance. Mom makes picnic food.

1. What strong words could be used to describe the plastic pool?
2. What strong words could be used to describe the sand castles?
3. What strong words could describe the music, the dancing, and the food?

B. Now revise the draft by adding strong words that create a clearer picture in readers' minds.

____

____

____

____

____

____

____

____

____

Name ____

Elena used text evidence from two different sources to respond to the prompt: *Write a dialogue between Omakayas and Little Bee about what they heard during the adults' conversation.*

"Did you get what you wanted from that big pile of gifts?" Little Bee asked as she happily played with her new doll.

"Yes, I did," Omakayas replied. She hesitated and said, "But I am troubled."

"Why are you troubled? You won the game of silence."

At that moment, Omakayas's grandmother brought them bowls of wild rice to eat. "I'm troubled by what the adults were saying. They said that we will have to move soon. There are new settlers coming that want this land. I don't want to leave here," Omakayas said trying not to cry.

"I didn't understand what they were saying, but they seemed so serious. Where will we go?" asked Little Bee.

"I am not sure. Father and the others kept speaking about something called a reservation. I am not sure what that means."

"Will we be able to grow wild rice there? How can we move somewhere if we can't grow wild rice there?"

"I don't know," answered Omakayas, with tears streaming down her cheeks.

Reread the passage. Follow the directions below.

1. **Circle** an example of a strong verb used by Elena.
2. **Draw a box** around a line of dialogue that Little Bee says.
3. **Underline** the text evidence that helps you make an inference that Little Bee got the gift she wanted.
4. **Write** two adverbs that Elena uses on the line below.

____

Name ______________________________

eldest	detested	ignored	treacherous
refuge	obedience	discarded	depicts

Use a word from the box to answer each question. Then use the word in a sentence.

1. **What is a way to say "shows in pictures or words"?** ______________

   ____

2. **What might a person seek during a bad storm?** ______________

   ____

3. **What is another word for *oldest*?** ______________

   ____

4. **What word might describe the things you find in a garbage can?**

   ____

5. **What is a dog usually rewarded for?** ______________

   ____

6. **How might your sister feel if you did not pay attention to her?** ______________

   ____

7. **What is another word for something that is disliked very much?**

   ____

Name ______________________________

Read the selection. Complete the theme graphic organizer.

Detail

↓

Detail

↓

Detail

↓

Theme

Name ______________________________

Read the passage. Use the reread strategy to make sure you understand what you read.

The Lost Diary of Princess Itet

Amelia peered down at the papyrus scrolls laid on the table. She
12 was standing inside a room full of them. They were bundled up
24 in rolls and spread over long tables. Strange symbols were drawn
35 on them in black ink. One looked like a bird. Another looked like
48 an open eye. The Egyptian hieroglyphs didn't look at all like the
60 English alphabet. She recognized the symbol *leb* that meant *heart.*
70 "Amelia, what are you doing?" Amelia's mother asked.
78 Amelia's mother was an archaeologist. She still had dust on her
89 clothes from digging in the pyramid that morning. It was 1905 and
101 exciting things were happening in Egypt. Amelia's mother and her
111 team of archaeologists found new artifacts every day.
119 "I'm reading the hieroglyphs," she said proudly.
126 "I bet you've learned a lot of new things from Mr. Breasted,"
138 her mother said. James Henry Breasted was her mother's boss and
149 Amelia's teacher. He knew a lot about ancient Egypt.
158 "Mom, do you think I could help your team at the pyramids?"
170 "I don't know, Amelia. Maybe when you're older," she said.
180 Amelia sighed and went back to reading the scrolls.
189 "Hello, Amelia," Mr. Breasted said. He walked up to Amelia,
199 smiling. "Are you translating the new papyrus scrolls we found?"
209 "I'm trying, but I don't know all of the symbols," said Amelia.
221 "Well, why don't we work on it together?" he suggested.
231 Amelia copied all the hieroglyphs on a piece of paper. Then
242 they translated each symbol into English. Soon they had translated
252 all the scrolls. Amelia read their finished work aloud.

Name ____

Day 32, the harvest season

I asked Mother if I could go to Pharaoh's feast. She said I am not old enough. The trip through the desert is long. I am nine years old! My cousins are going and they're the same age as I am. Last year my cousin Nefer talked about the delicious dessert for days. I wish there was a way to change Mother's mind.

Day 34, the harvest season

This morning Nefer had an idea. "Itet, you need to show your mother you can be useful at the harvest feast," she said. I'm a good writer, but I'm not sure if that will help.

Day 37, the harvest season

I have exciting news! I wrote a poem for Pharaoh. I tried very hard to write it from my heart. Mother loved it. She wants me to read it to Pharaoh at the feast. It will be a gift from our family. Nefer was right. I just needed to show her! And just in time too. We leave for the feast in an hour!

"Wow. It's a diary!" said Amelia.

"Not just any diary," said Mr. Breasted. "This is the lost diary of Princess Itet! Itet met the Pharaoh's son at this feast. They later married. Thank you, Amelia. I could not have done this without your help." Amelia had a sudden idea.

"Mr. Breasted, could I show these papers to my mom?"

"Of course! You earned it." Amelia ran off to show her mom.

"You helped translate *all this*?" her mom asked. "This is very good work, Amelia. Maybe you are ready to help at the pyramids."

"Thank you, Mom!" said Amelia.

And thank you too, Nefer and Itet, she thought.

Name ______________________________

A. Reread the passage and answer the questions.

1. What does Amelia want to do in the beginning of the passage?

____

____

2. What does Amelia do to help get what she wants?

____

____

3. What is the theme of this story?

____

____

____

B. Work with a partner. Read the passage aloud. Pay attention to intonation. Stop after one minute. Fill out the chart.

	Words Read	–	Number of Errors	=	Words Correct Score
First Read		–		=	
Second Read		–		=	

Name ______________________________

August 23, 1886: Arrival in America

My brother Pavol woke me up this morning. He shoved me and whispered loudly in my ear, "Aleksy! Wake up! We're almost there!" I rubbed my eyes, got out of bed, and followed him up on deck.

Once we had pushed our way through the crowd we were able to look out over the harbor for ourselves. I couldn't believe the sight that I saw! A giant statue the color of dull gold stood before the city. Workers crawled all over it like tiny ants.

Answer the questions about the text.

1. How do you know this text is historical fiction?

____

2. How is the story told?

____

3. Is Aleksy a historical figure or a fictional character?

____

4. Why do you think the author chose to tell this story in the form of a diary entry?

____

____

Name ____

Read each sentence below. Underline the context clues that help you understand the meaning of each homophone in bold. Then write the correct definition of the homophone on the line.

1. "I bet you've learned a lot of **new** things from Mr. Breasted," her mother said.

____

2. Last year my cousin Nefer talked about the delicious **dessert** for days.

____

3. I wrote a poem for Pharaoh. I tried very hard to **write** it from my heart.

____

4. I brought the pencils! And I brought some paper, **too**.

____

5. We leave for the feast in an **hour**!

____

Name ____________________

A. Complete each sentence by filling in the blank with the correct homophone in parentheses ( ). Use context clues to help you.

1. The baker rolls the **(doe, dough)** __________ before twisting it into the shape of a pretzel.

2. Do you know **(whose, who's)** __________ coming to the party this evening?

3. I must get to the **(root, route)** __________ of the problem if I want to solve it.

4. The heavy **(bolder, boulder)** __________ tumbled off the mountain into the valley below.

5. I didn't like the **(moose, mousse)** __________ because it made my hair feel sticky.

6. She had to **(wade, weighed)** __________ into the shallow pond to get her kite.

B. Read each word. Write the base word and suffix on the lines.

	Base Word	Suffix
1. purify	__________	__________
2. cancellation	__________	__________
3. beautify	__________	__________
4. royalty	__________	__________
5. captivity	__________	__________
6. calculation	__________	__________

Name ______________________________

A. Read the draft model. Use the questions that follow the draft to help you organize ideas and events in the text.

Draft Model

Bring a gift to welcome your new neighbor. Tell your neighbor about your favorite places in town. Invite him or her to a community event, such as a concert in the park.

1. **Of the ways the writer describes to help a new neighbor, which would the writer do first?**

2. **Of the ways the writer describes to help a new neighbor, which would the writer do last?**

3. **What sequence words can be added to help put the sentences in logical order?**

B. Now revise the draft by organizing the ideas and events in the text using sequence words.

____

____

____

____

____

____

____

____

Name ______________________________

Zach used text evidence from two different sources to answer the prompt: *Like Henry Johnston, many Americans immigrated to Mexico. Write a diary entry from María Rosalia's point of view describing whether Mexico is becoming a melting pot, a salad bowl, or a stew pot.*

November 11

Wagons never stop rolling into Alta, California! Not many years ago, the only foreigners were a few sailors and trappers. Today, hundreds of farmers from Missouri have settled here.

Will they obey the laws of Mexico? Lupita does not think so! She does not think they will try to melt into our culture. She thinks this part of Mexico will be like a salad. "The Americans will be like tomatoes, sitting on top of Mexican lettuce," Lupita says, her face turning as red as a tomato.

I understand how Lupita feels, but I am also a foreigner—or half of me is. That half might be Spanish, Russian, or American. I do not know which country's beliefs, language, or culture to try to hold on to. Would I be happier if I knew?

Foreigners like Henry Johnston could help California become an even better place. He respects Mexican laws and culture but also honors his American background. California could be like a stewpot filled with many different but delicious ingredients.

Reread the passage. Follow the directions below.

1. **Circle** an example of a simile in Zach's closing paragraph.
2. **Draw a box** around a sequence phrase that shows the order of events.
3. **Underline** the figurative language that shows how Lupita feels.
4. **Write** an example of how Zach uses an adverb to compare.

____

Name ______________________________

converted	renewable	coincidence	efficient
incredible	consume	consequences	installed

Use the context clues in each sentence to help you decide which vocabulary word fits best in the blank.

The class settled in as Ms. Gibson wrote the assignment for the group project on the board: Being Green.

"Being Green? What does that mean?" asked Tiffany. "Do we need to paint ourselves?"

Ricky smiled. "No, Tiffany. It means being better to the environment. For example, we should try to ______________, or use, ______________ resources, or resources that can be restored."

"Ricky's right," said Ms. Gibson. "I want all of you to find a way to tell your friends and family the ______________ of our actions if we don't take care of the environment. It's important to let everyone know that we should be more ______________ and create as little waste as possible."

"My parents ______________ solar panels on our roof so that we can use power from the sun," said Lance. "The sunlight is ______________ into electricity by the panels."

"I think taking care of the environment should be something that we all think about and plan carefully. Saving the environment shouldn't be something that is just a ______________, or happens by chance," said Britney.

"It sounds like you all already know a lot about this topic," said Ms. Gibson. "Now, let's convince as many people as we can to feel the same way as we do. Being green should be something we actually do, not just an ______________ way of life that nobody can achieve."

"Let's all be green!" said Tiffany. The class applauded, eager to begin the project.

Name ______________________________

Read the selection. Complete the main idea and details graphic organizer.

Main Idea
Detail
Detail
Detail

Name ____

Read the passage. Ask and answer questions to understand new information in the text.

Energy from the Sea

As I sat on the beach the other day, I saw the power of the waves
16 crash on the sand. The water splashed around me. Then the water
28 pulled along the shells that lay around me. This got me thinking.
40 We can use the wind and the sun to make power. We can use water,
55 too. Waterpower is also a renewable resource. It should be able to
67 help us solve our energy problems.

73 Waterpower has been in use for thousands of years. The earliest
84 use of hydropower can be traced to the waterwheel. It is a big wheel
98 with paddles on the rim. The force of the water turns the wheel. Then
112 the wheel runs machinery that is linked to it. Ancient Egyptians
123 used river currents to turn wheels way back in 2500 B.C. The ancient
136 Greeks and Romans used hydropower, too. It survived all the way
147 through medieval times.

150 But waterpower has evolved since then. Way back in 1628, the
161 Pilgrims used it to grind corn in mills. But by the 1800s, hot steam
175 replaced waterpower as the main power source. People used burning
185 coal to heat water. The boiling water then produced steam, which
196 ran engines and other machines.

201 By the end of the 1800s, waterpower came back into fashion.
212 Demand rose for electric energy. In 1882, the first hydroelectric plant
223 was built in Appleton, Wisconsin. It could make enough energy to light
235 a house and two paper mills. That's not much if you think about it. But
250 it was a start! As time went on, the demand for hydropower steadily
263 increased. One power plant now has the capacity of 7,600 megawatts.

Name ____________________

How Dams Work

You may think dams just hold water. But some dams are used to make waterpower. The amount of power they make depends on the height of the water. When the water is high, more pressure is put on the turbines down below. The more the turbines turn, the more power there is.

But there is a problem with hydropower. It is only useful in certain parts of the country. If there is not a large moving water source, then hydropower will not work. This is why some people believe waterpower is all nonsense. But there are states that do make lots of hydropower. Areas in California and the Pacific Northwest produce the most power.

I went to the library to find out how much of our energy comes from waterpower. About 7.8 percent of the power made in the United States is from hydropower. To my disbelief, a lot comes from fossil fuels and nuclear power, too. I had hoped to see higher numbers for renewable resources.

Perhaps one day we can learn to rely just on renewable resources. Look at countries like Brazil and Iceland. Iceland relies on geothermal power from hot springs. Brazil has one of the biggest dams in the world. These countries can give us a preview of how the United States can become a greener nation.

Name ____

A. Reread the passage and answer the questions.

1. What are three key details in paragraph 2?

____

____

____

2. How are these details connected?

____

____

3. What is the main idea of the whole passage?

____

____

B. Work with a partner. Read the passage aloud. Pay attention to expression. Stop after one minute. Fill out the chart.

	Words Read	–	Number of Errors	=	Words Correct Score
First Read		–		=	
Second Read		–		=	

Name ______________________________

Cooling our Homes

After electric fans came air conditioning. This kind of cooling had a big impact on how houses were built in America. Rooms became smaller so they would be easier to cool. Ceilings were lowered. Glass doors and picture windows replaced open porches.

Air conditioning also allowed cities to grow in new places. Harsh local climates no longer kept people from building comfortable homes. Desert cities like Phoenix, Los Angeles, and Las Vegas grew quickly after air conditioning was invented.

Dates in the History of Air Conditioning

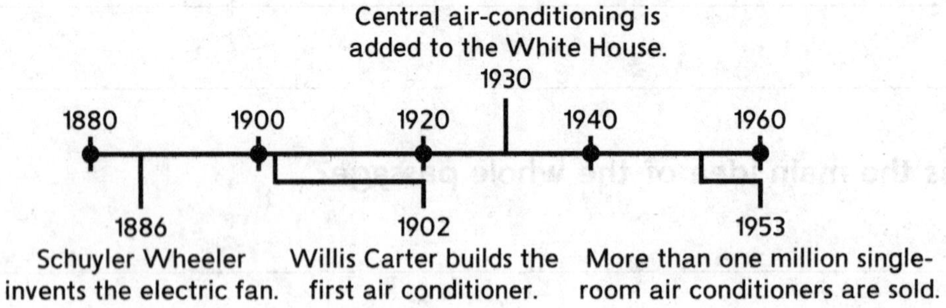
Central air-conditioning is added to the White House.
1930
1880
1900
1920
1940
1960
1886
Schuyler Wheeler invents the electric fan.
1902
Willis Carter builds the first air conditioner.
1953
More than one million single-room air conditioners are sold.

Answer the questions about the text.

1. How can you tell that this text is narrative nonfiction?

____

2. What text features are included in this text?

____

3. How does the time line help you understand the text?

____

____

Name ______________________________

Latin Prefix	Meaning	Greek Prefix	Meaning
non-	not	*hydro-*	water
pre-	before	*pre-*	before
		mega-	large
		geo-	earth

Read each sentence. Write the meaning of each word in bold on the line provided. Use the information about prefixes in the box above to help you.

1. The chapter **preview** in our book told us we would be studying marine life next week.

____

2. **Megawatts** are a greater unit of power than a watt.

____

3. Some ancient civilizations used rivers to create **hydropower**.

____

4. My friends looked at me in **disbelief** when I told them I met a movie star.

____

5. The **geothermal** temperature is hotter near Earth's core.

____

6. Some people used to think it was **nonsense** to say Earth was round!

____

Name ______________________________

A. Read each sentence. Circle the words that have prefixes. Write the prefixes on the line.

1. My teacher was disappointed when she learned that I had misplaced my work.

______________ ______________

2. One misstep and the mountain goat could fall from the rocky cliff.

____

3. I was uncertain if the disc was mislabeled because it had an odd title.

______________ ______________

4. I have never uncovered such silly nonsense in my entire life!

______________ ______________

5. Never discourage your friends from trying new and interesting things.

____

B. Read the words in the box below. Then read each definition of a word from mythology. Write a word from the box next to each definition to show that the two are related. Use each word from the box only once.

chronology	fortune	panic	titanic	hydrant	typhoon

1. Typhon – a dangerous monster ______________
2. Pan – a frightening creature ______________
3. Cronos – god of time ______________
4. Titans – gigantic gods ______________
5. Hydra – a water snake ______________
6. Fortuna – the goddess of luck ______________

Name ______________________________

A. Read the draft model. Use the questions that follow the draft to help you think about what transition words you can add.

Draft Model

Gas has many important uses. People use gas to power their cars and to run buses and trains. I think people need to save energy. People should stop using so much gas.

1. What transition word would show that the second sentence is an example of the idea in the first sentence?

2. What transition word would show that the ideas in the second and third sentences are related?

3. What transition word would show a cause-and-effect relationship between the ideas in the last two sentences?

B. Now revise the draft by adding transition words to link ideas.

____

____

____

____

____

____

____

Name ____

Kisha used text evidence from two different sources to answer the prompt: ***In your opinion, should people change the energy sources they use as conditions change?***

I think it's important that people change the energy sources they use as conditions change. As explained in *Energy Island*, one day nonrenewable sources of energy will not be available. Therefore, people should prepare for this change before it happens. Scientists are working on new ways to use renewable sources of energy. I think people should take advantage of that and start renewable energy projects to supply them with some or most of their energy.

Further, I agree with *Energy Island* that different places are good sources for different kinds of renewable energy. For example, a good place to collect solar energy would be in the desert. Wind energy works well in windy places like Denmark. People everywhere should find out what type of energy works best for the place they live in.

"Of Fire and Water" uses two myths to show how important energy is to people's survival. When there are no resources, such as fire or water, life is miserable. That's why we should not wait. We must plan to use renewable energy sources now and in the future.

Reread the passage. Follow the directions below.

1. **Circle** the sentence that states the author's opinion.

2. **Underline** one sentence that gives details that support Kisha's opinion.

3. **Draw a box** around two transition words.

4. **Write** two examples of a negative that Kisha uses on the lines below.

____

Name ____

currency	global	marketplace	entrepreneur
economics	invest	transaction	merchandise

Finish each sentence using the vocabulary word provided.

1. **(currency) In the United States** ____

   ____.

2. **(economics) Goods and services** ____

   ____.

3. **(global) Many businesses** ____

   ____.

4. **(invest) People say it is wise** ____

   ____.

5. **(marketplace) After the farmer harvests her corn,** ____________________________

   ____.

6. **(transaction) Paying dollars for a piece of fruit** ____________________________

   ____.

7. **(entrepreneur) With a new and creative idea,** ____________________________

   ____.

8. **(merchandise) At the shopping mall** ____

   ____.

Name ______________________________

Read the selection. Complete the main idea and details graphic organizer.

Main Idea
Detail
Detail
Detail

Name ______________________________

Read the passage. Use the ask and answer questions strategy to better understand key details in the text.

American Money

Think about a dollar bill. On it is an image of George Washington.
13 But Washington was not always on the dollar. And the dollar was not
26 always green. American money has changed over time.

34 Continental Currency

36 The American Revolution cost money. The colonists thought of a
46 way to pay for the war. They printed a kind of paper money. These
60 bills were called Continentals. But Continentals were not backed by
70 gold or silver. After the war they lost their worth.

80 A New Country, A New Currency

86 If at first you don't succeed try, try again. The United States
98 had won the war. Now they needed their own money. The dollar
110 became the United States unit of currency in 1785. The first United
122 States pennies were made in 1793. They were worth one cent each.
134 One hundred pennies equaled one dollar. The first pennies showed
144 a woman with flowing hair. She was called Lady Liberty. Today,
155 President Lincoln is on the penny. Other presidents are on our money
167 too. George Washington is on the quarter. Thomas Jefferson is on
178 the nickel. Andrew Jackson is on the $20 bill.

187 Honoring American Leaders

190 Ben Franklin was a famous author, scientist, and statesman.
199 He is on the $100 bill. Sacagawea was a Native American woman.
211 She helped Lewis and Clark reach the West Coast of North America.
223 She is on a special dollar coin.

Name ______________________________

Free Banking Era

A good name is better than riches. In 1836 most banks did not have good reputations. Any bank could print money called bank notes. Bank notes came in many colors, shapes, and sizes. A dollar note in Maine did not look the same as a dollar note in New York. Often bank notes could only be turned in for coins at the bank that made them. Some banks did not have gold or silver to back them up. There is a proverb that says, "Don't put all your eggs in one basket." Many people only had dollars from one bank. Soon people had dollars that they could not use.

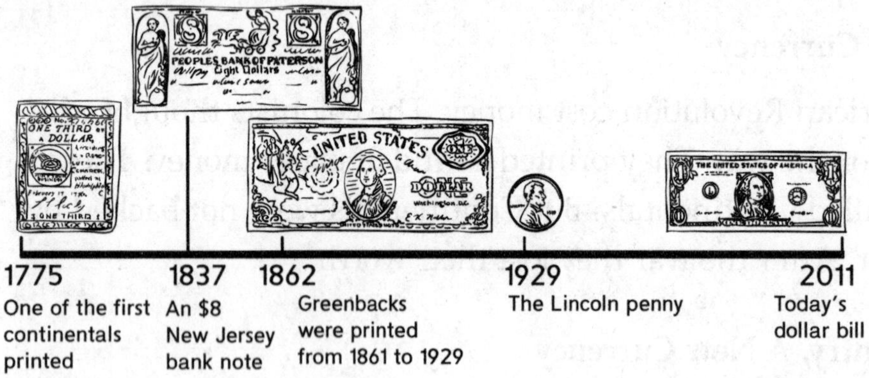

Greenbacks

In 1861 the first greenbacks were made. These notes used green ink. They were the same in all the states. $5, $10, and $20 bills were the first greenbacks. Later, $1, $2, $50, $100, $500, and $1000 bills were printed too. The faces of presidents were shown on them. George Washington was on the dollar bill for the first time in 1862. The North used greenbacks during the Civil War. The South used their own paper money called Confederate dollars. History repeats itself. Just like Continentals, Confederate dollars lost their worth when the war ended.

American Money Today

The Federal Reserve is in charge of printing money today. In 1929, it started printing smaller dollars. We still use these dollars today. Our money has changed over time. Who knows what the dollar will look like in 100 years!

Name ______________________________

A. Reread the passage and answer the questions.

1. What are two key details in paragraph 3?

____

____

2. What kind of money was being printed during the Free Banking Era?

____

____

3. Name two key details from the section called "Greenbacks."

____

____

4. What is the main idea of the whole passage?

____

____

B. Work with a partner. Read the passage aloud. Pay attention to accuracy. Stop after one minute. Fill out the chart.

	Words Read	–	Number of Errors	=	Words Correct Score
First Read		–		=	
Second Read		–		=	

Name ______________________________

Where Does *Dollar* Come From?

We use dollars all the time, but where does the name come from? The word dollar actually comes from an older word, *thaler*, and its spelling has changed over time. Thalers are silver coins once widely used throughout Europe. They got their name from the place where the silver was mined, Joachimsthal, a town in what today is the Czech Republic. At first, these coins were called Joachimsthaler, but this long name was shortened to become *thaler*.

GLOSSARY
Thaler
any of numerous silver coins once used in some Germanic countries

Answer the questions about the text.

1. How can you tell that this is an expository text?

____

2. What topic does the text tell you about?

____

3. What text feature is included? What does it tell you?

____

____

4. Where does the word *dollar* come from?

____

Name ____

Read each passage. Underline the paragraph clues that help you understand the meaning of each proverb or adage in bold. On the line, write the meaning of the proverb or adage.

1. The colonists printed a kind of paper money. They were called Continentals. But Continentals were not backed by gold or silver. After the war they lost their worth. **If at first you don't succeed try, try again**. The United States had won the war. Now they needed their own money. The dollar became the United States unit of currency in 1785.

____

2. Some banks did not have gold or silver to back them up. There is a proverb that says, "**Don't put all your eggs in one basket**." Many people only had dollars from one bank. Soon people had dollars that they could not use.

____

3. The South used their own paper money called Confederate dollars. **History repeats itself**. Just like Continentals, Confederate dollars lost their worth when the war ended.

____

Name ______________________________

A. Sort the words in the box below based on their suffixes.

sorrowful	tasteless	certainly	happiness
hairy	fitness	handful	wireless

-ful	*-less*	*-ness*	*-y/-ly*
1. ________	3. ________	5. ________	7. ________
2. ________	4. ________	6. ________	8. ________

B. Read the definitions below. Then read each word and circle the Greek or Latin root. Write the meaning of the root on the line.

The Greek root *astr* or *aster* means "star."

The Greek root *log, logo,* or *logy* means "word, topic, or speech."

The Latin root *port* means "carry."

The Latin root *vis* or *vid* means "see."

1. portable ______________________
2. video ______________________
3. asteroid ______________________
4. dialogue ______________________
5. visible ______________________
6. apology ______________________

Name ____

A. Read the draft model. Use questions that follow the draft to help you think about what content words you can add.

Draft Model

It is important to work. When you work, you make money. This allows you to pay for things you need. Working teaches you to be responsible. It is a way to help society.

1. How do the words used in this model help you understand the main topic?
2. What word could be used to better explain what the writer means by "work"?
3. Where could the writer include words like *income* to help the reader better understand what the topic is about?

B. Now revise the draft by adding content words to help explain more specifically the importance of work.

____

____

____

____

____

____

____

____

Name ______________________________

Hassan used text evidence from two different sources to answer the prompt: ***How do the laws of supply and demand affect Pedro's grain milling business?***

In *The Big Picture of Economics,* David Adler explains how supply and demand are connected. As supply goes up, prices go down, and as supply goes down, prices go up. As demand goes up, prices go up, and as demand goes down, prices go down. In "The Miller's Good Luck," Pedro's supply is the amount of grain he can mill. At first, when he is poor, Pedro can't mill much grain. So there isn't much demand for his work. Later, when Pedro makes some money, he invests it in his mill and makes it larger. All the farmers begin to bring their grain to Pedro's mill. Demand for his work goes up, so Pedro could probably charge more money for his work. On the other hand, since he can mill more grain and his supply is also up, Pedro might decide to lower his price. Whichever choice Pedro makes, he will probably be successful. He invests in his business, and he works hard.

Reread the passage. Follow the directions below.

1. **Circle** one of the transition words in the paragraph.

2. **Draw a box** around a detail about the mill that comes from "The Miller's Good Luck."

3. **Underline** two content words Hassan used to help explain the topic.

4. **Write** three prepositions Hassan used on the line below.

____

Name ______________________________

gobble	mist	individuality	roots

Use a word from the box to answer each question. Then use the word in a sentence.

1. What do both your family and a tree have in common? ______________

____

2. What is another word for "eat very quickly"? ______________

____

3. What is created when you spray a bottle of glass cleaner? ______________

____

4. When you show how you are different from others, what do you show?

____

____

Name ______________________________

Read the selection. Complete the theme graphic organizer.

Detail

↓

Detail

↓

Detail

↓

Theme

Name ______________________________

Read the poem. Pay attention to details that help you understand the author's message.

Me, As a Mountain

I am not an island.
5 On my worst day, I am

11 Florida, the ocean tempting me away from the mainland
20 states that are my parents.

25 On the days I feel best,
31 I am the Rocky Mountains,

36 broad as the landscape, filling a window.
43 I command any attention to the horizon.

50 I rise into the air, my hair a
58 mist against the blue of the sky.

65 I rest on the Great Plains.
71 Plateaus and pine forests lift me.

77 They are my parents'
81 broad shoulders I stand on.

86 I try to use them wisely to build
94 myself
95 into a tower of rock, strong and
102 impossibly tall.

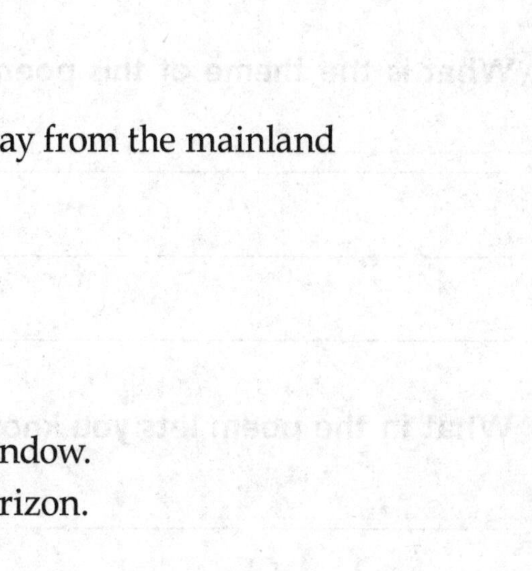

Name ____

A. Reread the passage and answer the questions.

1. What is this poem about?

____

____

2. What is the theme of this poem?

____

____

____

3. What in the poem lets you know what the theme is?

____

____

____

B. Work with a partner. Read the passage aloud. Pay attention to phrasing. Stop after one minute. Fill out the chart.

	Words Read	–	Number of Errors	=	Words Correct Score
First Read		–		=	
Second Read		–		=	

Name ______________________________

Quiet Room

I love the quiet of my room,
silent but for the slightest sound of a breeze that stirs the curtains.

Some friends I have would scoff and say,
"Come on, this place is boring!
Where's the music? Where's the fun?"

But me, I like a place to think–
a place where I can share my thoughts with only me
and let my mind wander out the window to the wide, wide world beyond.

Answer the questions about the text.

1. **What makes this text a free verse poem?**

____

2. **Are the lines in this poem regular or irregular?**

____

3. **What does the speaker of the text like about the bedroom? What do the speaker's friends not like about it?**

____

____

____

Name ________________________________

Imagery is the use of specific language to create a picture in a reader's mind. **Personification** is giving human qualities to a non-human thing.

Read the lines of the free verse poem below. Then answer the questions.

Me, As a Mountain

I am not an island.
On my worst day, I am

Florida, the ocean tempting me away from the mainland
states that are my parents.

On the days I feel best,
I am the Rocky Mountains

broad as the landscape, filling a window.
I command any attention to the horizon.

1. What is an example of imagery in this poem?

____

____

2. Point out an example of personification in this poem.

____

____

3. Write another stanza that includes imagery and personification.

____

____

____

____

Name ______________________________

Read each passage. Underline the metaphor in the passage. Then write the two things that are being compared on the lines.

1. On the days I feel best, I am the Rocky Mountains,

____

____

2. On my worst day, I am Florida, the ocean tempting me away from the mainland

____

____

3. I rise into the air, my hair a mist against the blue of the sky.

____

____

Name ______________________________

A. Read each sentence. Circle any words that have prefixes or suffixes.

1. I happily prepaid for the new book that will arrive in the store next month.

2. Do not prejudge the witness and reverse your ideas about what went on.

3. This establishment has been unchanged in its appearance for years.

4. The driver became fearful when she saw the two roads begin to intersect.

5. My semiweekly visits to the doctor were finally over.

B. Read the words from English in the box below. Then read each word from another language in bold. Write the word from the box next to its similar word from another language.

waffle	iceberg	lagoon	pretzel	macaroni	canyon

1. **brezel** (German) ____________________

2. **ijsberg** (Dutch) ____________________

3. **cañon** (Spanish) ____________________

4. **laguna** (Italian) ____________________

5. **makkaroni** (Italian) ____________________

6. **wafel** (Dutch) ____________________

Name ______________________________

A. Read the draft model. Use the questions that follow the draft to help you think about what concrete and descriptive details you can add.

Draft Model

I'm not very TALL at all
My hair is a MESS when I get out of bed
I like to display my collections
I always SING in the back seat of our car
My family is the BEST

1. What descriptive detail would tell how tall the speaker is?
2. What descriptive details would show how the speaker's hair is messy?
3. What concrete details would tell what the speaker collects?
4. What concrete details would tell what kinds of songs the speaker sings?

B. Now revise the draft by adding concrete supporting details that help build a clearer picture for readers.

____

____

____

____

____

____

____

Name ______________________________

Grace wrote the paragraph below to answer the prompt: *Reread "Birdfoot's Grampa" and "Growing Up." In your opinion, which poet is more successful in their use of imagery?*

I think that the poet of "Birdfoot's Grampa" is more successful in his use of imagery because it appeals to my sense of sight and touch. I felt like I was right there with the characters. The poet describes the little toads that are leaping around on the road as "live drops of rain." In the third stanza, the poet describes the old man's hands as, "leathery hands full / of wet brown life. " I can visualize the scene on the side of the road more easily than I can picture the scraped knees in "Growing Up." The poem, "Growing Up," doesn't use as many precise words so I can't picture a "house built on love." The words of "Birdfoot's Grampa" show me the old man's love and respect for nature. It is the many sensory details in "Birdfoot's Grampa" that allow me to visualize the old man standing in the rain holding the tiny toads.

Reread the passage. Follow the directions below.

1. **Circle** Grace's opinion statement.
2. **Draw a box** around an example of imagery that Grace uses as a supporting detail.
3. **Underline** a reason that Grace gives for why "Growing Up" does not have a lot of imagery.
4. **Write** two prepositions that Grace uses on the line below.

____